Prohibition, Prostitution and Presbyterian Pews

*An Irreverent, Outrageous, Heartwarming
Collection of Memories and Washington State History*

ROBERT W. KENNICOTT

With Jan Pierson

For information contact:

WildWest Publishing
P O Box 11658
Olympia, WA 98508

Printed in the United States of America
by Gorham Printing, Rochester, Washington
Cover design by Katy Keeslar
www.keeslarcreative.com

ISBN 978-09721800-9-5

http://www.calamityjan.com

Dedicated to
The Kennicott Family
with love and thanks for the memories.

FOREWORD

I have known the Kennicotts for most of my life. When my husband and I moved to Chehalis in the early 1960's, Florence and Bob Kennicott were already *Grandma and Grandpa Kennicott* to our children because my sister lived in Chehalis and our families were well acquainted. Our family still holds fond memories of the days and years on Kennicott Hill. With Florence by his side as wife, best friend, typist and editor, Bob—as he was called by most—wrote a few short books of his memories through the years, some of which I edited. His unusual 'voice' flew off every page and brought all of us into his heart-warming, eccentric world. His stories brought him close to our hearts. We continued to interact through the years. He became "Salty Bob" in my first mystery series for young readers; *The Carson Kids Mysteries.* His salty, sassy character infiltrated my stories as he had infiltrated and seasoned our lives through the years. In 1986 I moved to Olympia and it wasn't long before Florence and Bob settled into a retirement-assisted living facility near where I lived. It was there during the late afternoon of their lives that they handed me this collection of Bob's memories.

"Someday, see if you can do something with these, Jan," Florence, the family historian and recorder, said to me one day. "I have worked so many, many hours on this record. With my blindness and my dimming mental capacity, it seems to me the more I do, the farther I get behind."

Being a writer and storyteller myself, I had always loved listening to Bob's stories, especially since some got better with each telling. But this was different. I laughed and I cried as I often did when I read his words, but this time I knew I held a treasure in my hands. I knew I would share this memoir one day, but I wasn't ready yet. Maybe Chehalis and Lewis County weren't either. I set the collection on a shelf and let it rest. How could I keep his voice and those heart-wrenching memories intact and still keep it G-Rated and Lewis-County-Historical-Museum-ready? I couldn't. Bob Kennicott didn't grow up in a G-Rated world. He grew up next to the Great Northern Railroad tracks amidst the brothels and saloons of Chehalis and although his father, Dr. Guy William Kennicott was one of Lewis County's earliest doctors, young Robert was never spared the harsh realities of a rugged town caught between brothels and moonshine and loneliness.

To me, he was precious and impossible and I loved him dearly, and I suppose that's why I'm glad I picked up this collection of memories finally and began to juggle and shape it into a cohesive work, adding excerpts from his father's journals, dates and details that would help the reader stay on board. In the final distillation and as a disclaimer, however, I must state that the opinions and experiences are those of Robert William Kennicott and his alone and I take no responsibility if his words or experiences should offend some. This memoir, after all, came through his own unique filter and life journey. I'm honored to finally share this unorthodox treasure with a town I grew to love because a man named Robert Kennicott and his amazing wife, Florence, had a vision beyond the bricks and boardwalks of time and memory.

Jan Pierson

2012

CHAPTER 1

EARLY BEGINNINGS

Back in the year of 1904 I arrived in Chehalis, a belated present to my mother and father who had put in many difficult hours producing this gem. There are two stories about my advent into this vale of tears. My mother said it was an answer to prayer. My father had several other versions. Nevertheless on a warm day in April, the twelfth to be exact, when the cherries were in bloom, I escaped from my hiding place and entered this harsh world. My parents were very fortunate their seed survived as I only weighed three and a half pounds and could fit quite nicely in a shoe box. My sister, Frances Caroline was about eleven at the time and was called from school to see her baby brother. After running all the way and coming in breathless, she saw the wizened bit of human flesh which she refused to accept as a brother.

I didn't care for my mother's milk nor for several other brands that appeared in different containers, but finally they found that Eagle Brand satisfied my needs, and I have been a high flyer ever since, with a few other preferred labels in due time.

We have the old saying "Truth can be stranger than fiction," which is how I got this far. My father, Guy William Kennicott was born on January 29, 1859, the son of a Chicago dentist, William Kennicott. I was named after his cousin Robert Kennicott (1835-1866) who was an American naturalist and founder of the Chicago Academy of Sciences. In 1853 Kennicott began collecting and cataloguing for the Smithsonian in Washington DC to gather specimens of flora, fauna and minerals in a survey of Alaska, (then called Russian North America) prior to its purchase. Curator Baird, discovering what a genius he had on his hands, talked him into the Russian America trip. Guy first met his famous cousin when he was three years old on the scientist-cousin's return from his first expedition in 1862.

My father grew up near Chicago. After graduating from Northwestern University and Rush Medical College in 1885, he served his internship in the free clinic for the poor in the slums of Chicago where he delivered babies, patched up knife and gunshot wounds from saloon brawls and anything else that came along in the late 1800's. His first real position was as doctor for a mining and railroad construction camp which was pushing north into the wild timber country of Wisconsin and Minnesota.

Guy Kennicott's Journal, July 3, 1886

Instead of the fashionable denizens of a great city I attend the rough miners in their log mining camps, breathe the clear, cold air of Lake Superior, walk miles over the wretched tote roads and carry my medicines in a satchel swung over my back. It is a strange practice and rough but I like it and eat my meals with a vigorous appetite off from tin plates in log cook shanties in the dark pine forests. I am content to sleep on a bed of fragrant hemlock boughs in a cabin or tent while in the dark distance the wolves howl a dismal chorus.

Many times a long ride, probably in the night, would end in a narrow trail through the dense timber to a little bare cabin in the forest. In such an environment I think I have found every form of trouble that a hilarious nightmare in its happiest moments could devise, from a ten day retained placenta with a temperature of 106 degrees and everyone in the house including the baby, in the full swing of smallpox to a strangulated

8

hernia with a foot of the gut gangrened, and my only assistant a man so drunk that he could not hold the cone after I had put the patient to sleep. There was not a vessel in that shack clean enough to boil water in, so I cut the top from a coal oil can and boiled a dirty sheet for dressings. I did an enterectomy by the smoky light of a little hand lamp with a broken chimney, tied him up and in the early morning, just as it was getting daylight, left him with his drunken neighbor to a diet of flap jacks, bacon and sour dough bread. Of course, I thought he would die, but he didn't.

In the settlement at railhead there was a telegraph operator by the name of Charlie Chamberlain and a saloon keeper by the name of John Graham. The three of them became acquainted, and while it was a casual acquaintance, they would meet later in Union City, where Dr. Kennicott migrated in 1889, the year Washington Territory became a State. Guy Kennicott was surprised to find these two men had also moved there and were running a telegraph station and a saloon.

My father met my mother, Harriet Foster Black in Union City while she was teaching high school and he was trying to establish his medical practice there. A friend of my father's at Rush Medical College had come west as a doctor for the Indian community of Tahuya. Dad had been captivated by his tales of the wonderful hunting and fishing in the virgin territory of Hood Canal in Washington Territory.

My mother, Harriet, was born in 1863 and raised in West Hebron, New York, receiving a classical woman's education which included course work in both Hebrew and Greek. She was a well educated woman for her time but because of her health, the family doctor advised her to get out of those severe northeastern winters and move west. After completing her degree she was hired at the teachers' college in Cheney, Washington but in 1890 while aboard the train coming west she was informed that the college had just burned down. Undaunted, due perhaps to her rock-ribbed Irish Presbyterian upbringing, she continued west anyway and found herself teaching high school near the town of Union City (now Union) along Hood Canal. It was there in Union City where my parents met and married in 1892 and a year later, my sister Frances Caroline Kennicott was born. My father, realizing he could not make a living in so small a town, bought out the practice of a Dr. J.S. Herndon in Chehalis and moved there in 1895.

Dr. Kennicott writes; *The country was rapidly developing, people were coming from all over this broad land to make their homes in this wonderful Washington. With the increase of population new conditions required change. Roads took the place of trails, bridges were built, and many could be reached on wheels. My stout, heavy, two-wheeled "shay," with its sturdy team and big side-lights, became well known about the country. Increasing demand, however, made it necessary that I should have some place to care for patients who could not be attended at their homes or at great distances. So I built a little hospital. Not much, only fifteen beds, but well equipped, with full trained nurses and a convenient, well-lighted operating room. This was the first hospital to be built in Lewis County, and enabled me to do work that without it I could not have done. Patients were brought on rude, homemade stretchers, a blanket, or a few gunny sacks over rough poles. Then, as roads improved, other means were employed. But the people were being educated to the advantage of the hospital, and in a very short time I was relieved of much of my long distance work and giving far better service than it had been possible to give under former conditions.*

The Kennicott home and office were on a half city block just west of the railroad tracks near what used to be the center of town. In 1903 they built the hospital. Both house and hospital covered the city block bounded by Center, State and Prindle Streets and backed by the railroad.

Several years later, Dr. Kennicott discovered that Charlie Chamberlain had become a telegraph operator in Chehalis and eventually Mr. Graham also moved here to run a saloon, each man acting independent of the other. All three of these men remained in Chehalis until their deaths.

Growing up, I had a nodding acquaintance with John Graham, but Charlie was a garrulous old soul and when he saw me coming down the street he would start laughing as he came up to me. "Did I ever tell you about your dad when we were in Minnesota?" and off he would go on a tale I had heard from him many times before.

One of his favorites was of the time he told my Dad there had been an explosion at one of the camps above railhead. Although it was late, Dad put saddlebags of instruments and medicines on his horse and took off at a gallop. About five miles out of town a shot rang out and the horse fell. Dad kicked his feet out of the stirrups and rolled off the grade into the ditch and watched. Two men came up the other side from where the horse was. They were laughing and talking about how easy it had been to knock over the pay master, but when they took the saddle bags off of the horse, Dad stuck them up with a gun in each hand. He made them drop their guns and start walking towards town, then took their two horses and continued on his way. After their long walk back into town, the two men went into the saloon and told what had happened to them. They had been held up by that little half-pint doctor, disarmed and made to walk back on foot. Everyone in town thought it hilarious since Dr. Kennicott was a little man, short and slight of build and known throughout camp as a "tenderfoot."

In the early 1900's our one-man police force in Chehalis consisted of a night watchman who patrolled the streets, checking on unlocked doors and on strangers wandering the streets at night. He was a little man about 5'4" tall, stooped and wore a Colt 45 on his leg and carried a night stick. In spite of all this, he commanded the respect of everyone from mayor to the toughest logger.

There was a logger who had lost the most of his right arm. He still

11

was one hell of a man in the woods, though. That one arm was better than the two of most anyone else and Saturday night was usually his night to howl. More often than not, he ended up trying to take the Greek pool hall apart. The Greeks would call the night watchman, but this little one-man police force would go up to him and say, "Come along now, or I'll have to hurt you."

The big ox would reply, "Okay, John, let's go." And he would spend the night in the pokey, sober up and be turned loose in the morning.

The poorly illuminated streets of Chehalis were safe both day and night. Women were safe at all times. In those days a rapist would have had a short life.

CHAPTER 2

THROUGH THE BIG EARS
OF A LITTLE BOY

My education started early. When I first knew Chehalis, it was the proud possessor of seven churches and fourteen saloons. The churches had locks on their doors, the saloons didn't. The bat-winged doors swung both in and out and the only time they had locks on them was after the passing of the Volstead Act in 1919 when Prohibition was established during the time of the First World War.

When the men came in from the logging camps on Saturday night they spent their wad in the saloons, most of which had wood-planked floors splintered by many years of hob-nailed boots. If they were lucky they spent their money in an honest saloon of which there were very few. Tins of Copenhagen chew, jars and barrels of pickled eggs, sausages and other delicacies beckoned from behind the bar. Most of the loggers were addicted to nicotine and chewed because they were not allowed to smoke in the woods. The poor bastards went in, cashed their checks at the bar and were given a free drink, which very often was laced with a Mickey Finn. After two or three of these drugged drinks, they would pass out and were very nicely taken into a back room to sleep it off. They were fortunate to be in Chehalis instead of South Bend or Hoquiam because there, as rumor had it, when they passed out they could be dropped through a trap door to be swept out with the tide. Many men who came west in those days were never heard from again.

Come Sunday night in Chehalis, the bar keeper would wake the logger up, tell him what a good time he'd had, and how he had drunk up all his money. "But, here is a five-dollar gold piece which I'm giving you because you're a nice guy. You've sobered up now so go back to camp and work and come back here next Saturday because we look after you."

I learned all this through the big ears of a little boy. Many, many years later when one of these saloons was being torn down, I stood there watching and saw for myself the piles of empty Mickey Finn vials that had been dropped between the walls.

I'm told that soon after my entrance into the world, my mother went back to school teaching to augment the family income. She found a little girl whose father had been trying to sell her to a local shopkeeper and decided to rescue her by hiring her to look after me for a half day and go to school for the other half. This girl came from a Bohemian family. Her younger sister had a tubercular leg and my father opened up the bone, scraped it, washed it out and she lived to adulthood. Her older sister looked after her in the hospital and the younger one stayed on with our family to look after me.

In the afternoons I was cared for by an Indian woman who married a French Voyager.* I remember that she was a sweet, lovable person with a wrinkled face as soft as velvet. I loved to touch her cheeks and take the pins out of her hair and watch it fall loose around her face. Her husband would occasionally get drunk and beat her up for the amusement of it and often she would show up in our home with a split lip or black eyes. I remember kissing them and trying to make her feel better.

My mother was a large, powerful woman, a pillar of the church and an upholder of the morals of the town. In her hide-bound way she was determined to make an angelic Little Lord Fauntleroy out of me, while I was determined to prevent such a catastrophe. For many years she had her way. I wore a sailor suit with an eagle on one sleeve, a huge collar and patent leather pumps, and I wore long curls even after I started kindergarten. I was a cute little bastard. Even in the later years I was never allowed to wear big overalls like the rest of the boys. My mother, having come from New York State, always ordered my clothes from the National Cloak and Suit Company of New York. Some of these fashions died in the aborning, others withered and blew away on the Great Plains. The ones that survived the trip across the nation arrived about three years after they were fashionable in New York. But was I ever behind the times? Hell, no! I was the promulgator of fashions never seen before or since. You have no idea what that did to my sensitive little soul. Arriving at school with something new and different—something never seen or heard of by my contemporaries—wasn't what I called fun.

I spent most of my younger years in Kindergarten. The first one was in a little house that still stands at the corner of Prindle and St. Helens. The second one was on Adams Avenue behind where the Terrace Park Apartments are now. To get there I had to walk through the yard of Frank Powers. They had an English Bull dog who was built close to the ground and whose teeth always showed. The damn dog would stand in the walkway and terrorize me. My screams usually brought one of the family members out to tell me that he was very friendly. They never convinced me one bit.

My third shot at Kindergarten was in the parish house of the Episcopal Church on St. Helens Avenue. This was run by Ruth Dickson, daughter of the rector of the church. May Delight Palmer, Frances Power, Lucille Taylor, Vilva Cory, Kate, Clarrisa and Ben Burt Frost and several others whose names I have forgotten, were in the class. Aside from Ben Burt, I was the only male member of the kindergarten class. I used to wonder if one went directly from

15

kindergarten to college because I spent so many years in kindergarten. If I seem childish, it is only because I remain confused. Most of the children at that time began grade school at the age of six, but I was eight years old when I entered the first grade in the West Side school. Of course I was way ahead of the rest of the class in the use of scissors and paste.

While I was still in kindergarten my folks decided to remodel the house they had purchased from Dr. Herndon. This meant that they dug a big basement below it by hand, carrying out that blue clay bucket by bucket. And then they built a huge three-story, fifteen-room house above it and around it.

The architect was Ed Doyle who designed the Presbyterian Church in Chehalis, Reed College and a number of banks and public buildings along the coast from Portland to San Francisco. In the building nothing was too good or too expensive. They bought oak trees from a man in Toledo who hauled them to Chehalis where they were cut into tongue and groove floor boards. The polishing and filling all had to be done by hand. Each of the shingles on the side of the house was shaped and hand-dipped in creosote to give them an antique look. The pillars in the living room were turned on a lathe by the Wisconsin Timber Company in Littell. All this left my parents with a burden of debt that followed them the rest of their lives.

Politics weren't much more crooked then than now. One mayor of Chehalis got elected by hiring a surrey and driver to transport all of the town's prostitutes from one precinct to another so they could vote for him in each one. After he was elected, he bought one of the finest homes in town, on Pennsylvania Avenue. Before long, it became a slum. The front porch soon had a washing machine, sacks of cow feed and a bale or two of hay. The cow that they had brought to town with them soon made a shambles of the formal garden at the rear of the house.

Another mayor was one Dr. C......... In my opinion, he wasn't worth a damn as a doctor, but he was a very forward looking person—for himself at least. That was the time when Chehalis went up to the headwaters of the Newaukum River for pure mountain water and brought it down some twenty miles in wooden pipes manufactured in Chehalis. There was much talk of pay-offs to the mayor in getting the right-of-way and in the purchase of the pipe. All I know is that the good doctor came here penniless and left the county well off. Still, in spite of all the skullduggery, the damn thing worked.

Two railroad officials came by one day and Dr. Kennicott was asked to escort them to the advanced camp. In those days many people loaded their own shells. My dad had a bullet mold and also just for fun, he loaded some of the shells with bird shot. As he was taking the officials to the advanced camp, a grouse flew upon the limb of the tree. He pulled out his pistol and shot it dead on the first shot. The officials were very impressed, especially so when he did the same thing a second time. Dad did not think to tell them that the pistol was loaded with bird shot. When they arrived back at camp, the officials remarked about the doctor's skill with a pistol.

"Oh yes," they were told, "he's a crack shot and he has a very quick temper too. Watch out for that one."

It wasn't until several weeks later that Dad learned of the tales that had been spread about him. Finally he understood why those officials had been so polite and respectful.

CHAPTER 3

THE AMAZING DR. KENNICOTT

The first hospital in Lewis County was a frame house in Chehalis moved onto the lot next to our home at 1030 State Street. Later this was enlarged to a 15-bed capacity by adding a maternity wing and a four-bed ward. A kitchen and dining room downstairs were used by the nurses and at times by the Kennicott family. The hospital served the people of Lewis County for over twenty-five years until my father stopped operating it as a hospital although he continued using it for his professional offices until his retirement in 1942.

Guy Kennicott was a most talented individual, giving up a promising, potential career in art and music to take up medicine. He had a wonderful tenor voice which he never quite succeeded in losing, and had a natural flair for the playing of any instrument he set his heart to. He could sculpt and paint and with his wood-burning skill, he decorated beautiful boxes and tables which he had made by hand. Oil painting was also a favorite outlet and his oil painting of the Jackson Prairie Court House remains in the archives of the Lewis County Museum.

He also wrote at least three books of poetry, none of which was ever published. My mother called it "doggerel." Still, it seems that whatever he set out to do, he could do—if not brilliantly—at least better than most.

18

Dr. Kennicott was also one of those people who could read a book in a few hours since he had a photographic memory and could quote page numbers with specific facts and information. His flair for medical innovation and sense of compassion were offset by his lack of business management. Neither the hospital nor his practice ever made money. They were run to serve the sick and injured regardless of whether there was a possibility of being paid. Rooms were three dollars a day and the maternity ward was five dollars a day for those who could afford to pay.

There was one little girl with dropsy.* She was one of a family of many more children than loaves of bread which was probably one reason her father brought her to the hospital and abandoned her. She was a charming little thing with beautiful auburn hair and warm brown eyes. Every so often the fluid in her body had to be drained off. She was so patient during the painful process and afterward would be ill for a number of days. Then the sparkle would return and she was her charming self again. She lived at the hospital for years. Her family was never seen again and when she died, my parents buried her.

Another little country girl fell in the hole where her father was char-pitting a stump while clearing some land. She was so severely burned it was a question of survival. She lived in the hospital for months and months while Dr. Kennicott grafted skin on face, neck, shoulders and side. There was such a great surface to be covered that after he had exhausted the source of any human skin, he experimented successfully with the skin of frogs and chickens. Eventually most of her own skin finally grew back and she lived to marry and raise a family. My father never got so much as a thank you from the family.

It was during the construction of the original hospital in 1903 that Lewis County suffered its worst train accident. A special train was bringing delegates back from an Elks convention in Portland to their homes in Seattle and Tacoma. There was some talk that the engineer and fireman were drunk, but if not, they were the only ones on the train who weren't. Coming down the Napavine grade, the train jumped the tracks and there were many serious injuries.

My father was the Northern Pacific railroad doctor. Flat cars were sent from Centralia to the scene of the accident and the injured were laid on the open cars and brought directly to where the unfinished hospital was standing.

This was an emergency that called upon the unusual administrative ability of Mrs. Kennicott. While Dr. Kennicott gave life-saving services to people with severed arms and legs, my mother called in all the doctors and nurses available. Not content with that, she called on friends and neighbors to give a hand and to bring any blankets and supplies that were available.

The new un-hung doors of the hospital were used as stretchers to carry the wounded into the hospital from the flat cars on the tracks. The doors became so soaked with blood that later on, they could not be stained as originally planned, but had to be painted instead. All the rooms and hallways of the hospital were filled with the wounded. Since pain and anesthesia do not mix with alcohol, it is easy to imagine the chaotic and difficult conditions in which they had to work.

Mrs. Kennicott saw two blood-stained shoes on the back porch of the house and picked them up to throw them aside. They seemed heavy and when she looked inside, to her horror she saw two feet in them.

Frank Schuster, the section boss, came up with a woman's arm wrapped up in newspaper. Sensing it might be important later, they unwrapped it to see whether there was or had ever been a ring on that hand. There was no sign of her ever having worn one, so later when the family sued the railroad for the loss of a valuable diamond ring, two witnesses testified to the fallacy of their claim.

Our state was fortunate in that it was as far west as you could go without getting your feet wet. Besides the ambitious ones who answered the call of "Go West, Young Man," we were the recipients of all the misfits of the other states who came here for many reasons; some to escape the law, some to escape nagging wives and some merely because they had itchy feet. There were also "remittance men," those of good family in the old country who got a yearly stipend to stay away from home. There were a few Southern colonels left over from the Civil War and some characters who simply left home by popular demand. If someone told you where he came from, that was his business. You never asked. A riotous array of characters moved into Lewis County back then.

Before my parents moved from Union City to Chehalis, in fact before the advent of the white man, the virgin forests of Washington Territory extended from the summit of the Cascades to the Pacific Ocean. There were a few natural prairies and a number of burns either caused by lightning or Indians. As there is little or no sustenance for elk or deer in a heavy stand of firs, they were forced to migrate to burns or natural openings in the forest. The Catholic fathers settled at Cowlitz Landing and finding virgin prairie, planted wheat. Their first harvests were a hundred bushels to the acre or more. Most of the people who came west looking for land had no use for the huge fir trees, so felled them to clear the land. The easiest method was to bore a hole straight into the heart of the tree with another hole slanted down to meet the first. This made a fire hole and chimney. By lighting a bit of pitch in the lower hole, the fire was directed toward the heart of the tree and would eventually fell it. The body of the tree was eliminated in the same manner. Boring in from one side and down from the top about ten to fifteen feet apart burned the fallen tree completely.

With more people moving into Washington and Oregon and with the development of California where our timber was needed, sawmills sprang up everywhere, especially along the salt coast for easy shipping. When the South Bend line of the Northern Pacific Railroad was built, small lumbering towns sprang up every few miles along the line. As the timber was used up and the mills were abandoned, many of the towns were also. There were always a few that managed to survive as a general store, a post office and a smithy.

In the early days of few roads, pioneer doctors had to carry on much of their practice on horseback. On many a winter night I remember being awakened to the pounding of a horse at the stable door. Very soon Mr. Bailey, the stable boy would come to the door and lift my father off the horse, too cold and stiff to get off by himself. On some of those calls my father would have had to swim with his horse across the cold, swollen rivers. Back in the saddle, he would fall asleep exhausted and the horse would find his own way home.

On one such occasion in the dead of winter, my father was half awakened by the sound of his horse's hooves on what sounded like wood. The horse had taken a game trail for a shortcut home and had followed the trail over a snow-covered log above a deep chasm with a rushing stream far below. Dad gazed back and it made his blood run cold.

When Dr. Kennicott had calls from the far eastern end of the county he would often be gone for several days. Because there were no phones in the rural areas, word of mouth was the standard communication. People would hear that the Doctor was in the area, send him word or leave a lantern or a cloth on the road for him to follow the trail to their cabin. On one such occasion there was a telephone call for my father to go to a remote cabin but the relayed message was garbled and all he could get was that someone was sick. It was dark by the time he had taken the lantern turn through the woods. In a crude cabin he found a logger lying on a cot. His leg had been crushed in a logging accident several days before and gangrene had already set in. My father knew that if there was any hope of saving the man's life, amputation must be done immediately, but he brought only his medicine case. Quickly he found a carpenter's cross-cut saw and a butcher knife and together with the man's logging partner, built a hot fire and sterilized both in a five-gallon kerosene can. The only pain-killer on hand was whiskey and both men were already drunk when he arrived; one coping with the pain and the other frantic and helpless with sympathy for his friend. Giving the dying man another big shot of alcohol, my father tied him to the bed and with a lantern, a saw and a butcher knife; he amputated the man's leg.

About six months later a man came into my father's office and asked, "What do I owe you, Doc?"

"Who are you? I don't remember seeing you before." When Dad realized this was the man whose leg he had amputated by lantern light he almost fell off his chair. "If you lived through that, you don't owe me a damn cent."

Dr. Kennicott writes; *There were no telephones, and when a doctor was needed badly some neighbor got on his horse and came to town. He was cold and wet when he got in and usually took a few drinks to keep the cold out on the road back. The doctor saddled his horse, threw on the old saddle bags, a satchel over his shoulder for instruments, etc., then off into the storm, rain, sleet or snow, and night. Dark? One could not see his horse, let alone the road, plodding along through sloppy mud, over endless corduroy, then more mud, then a narrow trail with wet ferns horse-high, sometimes absolutely lost even when the man went back with you, then on 'till a little cabin is found. A shout, a sleepy half-dressed man or woman, and maybe you have gone five miles too far. Turn back and search the black walls on the sides of the road for the little opening where the trail comes in. You finally get there, a little shack in the clearing.*

No doubt or question as to your patient being sick, mighty sick, or they would not have sent for you. They had tried everything they knew, consulted the family doctor book from cover to cover. Now it's up to you to see him once or twice and cure him. If it's an operative case, don't for a moment think hospital. "There ain't no sich." Get out your anesthetic and instruments and operate under the soft light of a guttering candle or a sawed-off lamp. And for the after care? Well, for a few days at least he

will not care for food. After that he goes back to the old diet; flap jacks,
sour dough and the rest of it. Probably not a dollar in the house. You'll
get it though, all of it, every cent...sometime.

Then on the long road home in the morning you may be stopped half
a dozen times. They have heard that "Doc's been out to Jones' and they
are waiting at the side of the road to have you come in and see some of
their ailing ones. You'll probably eat dinner at one of these places. Same
old stuff; sour dough and hog meat. Then in the afternoon you get home
and learn that Sam Smith twenty miles away in another direction, has
broken his leg, tree fell on him, and away you go again. Good people,
kindly people, honest people. Some of the scenes seem humorous now as
I look back. They were serious enough then. We gave ourselves, all that
we had, the best that was in us. And so the days have crept silently away
and hidden themselves in the years. (REMINISCENCES OF A HALF
CENTURY OF PRACTICE. G.W. Kennicott, M.D. July, 1930)

In those days doctors didn't usually lounge around swimming
pools but they did fall into creeks and rivers now and then. On one
occasion when Dad was answering a call near the Gregg place west of
the Chehalis River near Adna, his horse and buggy had to cross the
river. There was a ford there, but because of heavy rains, the western
bank had washed away so when the horses tried to make the lunge to
get over the bank, the tongue stuck deep into the mud. The horses
went crazy, jumping and lunging half in the water and half under it.
Dad jumped into the river with pocket knife ready, cutting the traces
so they could get free from the buggy and jump to solid ground. The
Gregg men helped him pull the buggy out of the river, patched up
the harness and Dr. Kennicott was on his way.

When hop-raising was still a major crop in the Chehalis Valley
(where the Art Hamilton farms once stood), the Indians came by the
trainload to do the harvesting. They came from the Okanogan country bringing their families, horses, dogs and tepees.

One day the manager, Mr. Dobson came to Dad for help. He

explained that the Chief's baby was sick, the medicine man had been called in, and there was one hullabaloo going on while the hops were spoiling on the vine. Dad brought me along this time and since it was evening by the time we arrived, he tied up the horses and told me to wait for him in the buggy. He proceeded on down to the old log hop house where the Indians were assembled and making a commotion. Possibly due to the fact that I spent three years in kindergarten, I forgot that he had told me to stay in the buggy and instead slipped down to the dwelling and peeked through a nice-sized slat in the chinked logs.

My father knew their language and always got along well with the Indians. I watched while he gave the formal greeting to the Chief; smoking the tobacco pipe and blowing the smoke east, south, west and north and up and down. I saw the medicine man shaking a rattle and jumping around over the baby and the fire. His painted face and primitive gestures terrified me. My dad was the only white man there and when he went over to examine the baby, the medicine man jumped between them. Calmly, my father continued toward the baby. I was terrified, sure he would scalp Dad. Undeterred, my father pushed him to one side and picked the baby out of the cradle board, unwrapping the many blankets in the stifling heat of the hut. He stuck a finger in the baby's mouth and discovered it was simply trying to teethe. Taking a knife from his medicine bag, he lanced the child's gums, then took out a syringe filled with olive oil and gave it an enema, holding it out while it unloaded. He then took the baby over to the mother, pulled her dress open and immediately the baby began nursing.

At that moment there was a great sigh of relief from the whole group of Indians.

I was seven-years-old, smart enough to know I'd better make a beeline back to the buggy where I had been told to stay. When my father returned he said, "Well, how did you enjoy the show?" Before

I could protest he continued, "I saw your beady little eyes in the crack between the logs."

In those early days, my father had to rely on Indian ponies for his transportation. These were wild horses, shipped out in stock cars by the railroad for sale to the big packing companies. Dad chose two buckskins with black mane and tail for his daily use. They were small, but they were tough and served him well. To get over rough roads, he used a two-wheel cart, and stood on a step in the rear. There was a box that ran all the way across the cart from one wheel to the other which is where he kept all his medical and surgical equipment. There was also a low seat in the back where he could sit down when the going was easy.

Later he was able to buy three high-spirited Morgan horses: Jack, Princess and Tanglefoot. These Morgans were all riding as well as driving horses. Tanglefoot was one of those rare personalities that became legends in the families of their owners. My father bought him cheap because the horse had killed a man and was completely unmanageable. But he knew that a horse of his spirit would give excellent service once he was trained. When first he faced up to Tanglefoot, the horse was in a cage because no one dared go near him in a stall.

Dr. Kennicott stripped to his underwear and donned his tennis shoes, then entered the cage for the first lesson. His first job was to prove to Tanglefoot that he, a one-hundred twenty-five-pound man, was stronger than a thousand pound horse. When the horse came at him rearing, Dad caught a front foot and at the same time pushed with his shoulder so as to throw the horse off balance. Then Dr. Kennicott sat on his head and began patting him calmly and talking to him. A few minutes later he would start all over again. Each time the horse reared and came striking at him with his front hoofs, the process was repeated. After the third time, Dr. Kennicott called him to come to him. When he didn't come, my father stung the horse with the whip. With a few repetitions of this, Tanglefoot stood for awhile, and finally, cautiously walked up to him. After that the doctor had no trouble with the horse. To his dying day, Tanglefoot remained a loyal, one-man horse.

The other two Morgans were also trained to come when they were called. When the horses were in their forty-acre pasture, all Dr. Kennicott had to do was to whistle and clap his hands and they came running to him. Every summer each horse was given a month of freedom and rest in pasture.

When rivers and streams were high, Dad usually traveled to his calls on horseback. When he came to a place where there was no bridge, he would make a bundle of his clothes, fasten them as best he could to the horse's head to keep them dry, then holding on to the horse's mane, the two of them would swim the stream; he dressing on the other side. If called to the eastern end of the county, traveling by horseback was the only way he could get there, particularly in wintertime.

The saddle bags in which he carried his medicines and implements are now on exhibit in the Lewis County Historical Museum.

Dr. Kennicott writes; *We have forged on with inconceivable strides. Wonderful paved avenues have taken the place of the old corduroy. Machines flash along at high speed where but yesterday the slow horse, or the man with a pack on his back plodded along through endless mud. Distance is eliminated and we reach people over a vast area in a moment by telephone. We have reached an age of new things, an age of concentration, hospitalization in civic centers and splendid equipment. Our colleges are training men to be high-powered investigators in various lines, specialists rather than just doctors. Efficiency is the cry. Maybe we are overdoing it. This is a question that I have no doubt the doctor of tomorrow will be fully able to answer. (REMINISCENCES OF A HALF CENTURY OF PRACTICE. G. W. Kennicott, M.D. July, 1930)*

CHAPTER 4

LIFE ALONG THE TRACKS

When I was a wee lad, being so well situated with my home on the edge of the railroad, I spent much of my time watching the trains. This was back in the good old days of the six-day week and the ten to twelve-hour day. When the South Bend train whistled, I sneaked out our back gate and ran for the depot. The train had to stop for the brakeman to open the switch to the main line and then slow down so the brakeman could close the switch after the train was through and run to get onboard.

The little engine had to work hard to get up speed since the train was made up of freight cars, flat cars and lumber and logs in the gondolas. Many of the cars held large Douglas fir logs. At the rear of the train there was a car—the first half baggage, back half smoker, and at the end of the train there was a battered coach for passengers. Littell was the last stop before Chehalis so the conductor had to pick up fares from one town to the next. After the coach and a half, he had to use his caulk shoes to advantage as he worked his way forward on the train; he had to walk over boxcars, gondolas of logs and log cars with two small logs making a nest for a large one. Since the passengers were at the rear of the train, the front end was out of town before the coaches arrived at the depot.

In those days loggers spent the workweek boarding in the lumber camps that dotted the forested hills. It was fun watching them return home, working their way forward across the train cars which they did for two reasons; one, to escape paying fare to the conductor, but the most important was to be the first man to get his belly against the bar, get his paycheck cashed, and also to get the first drink. They hit the cinders on a dead run which carried them to the back door of the Big Mug, the Biggest Mug or the Mint. Once in awhile a man would lose his footing and go ass over a tin cup, but they never seemed to get hurt.

Another pleasing part of the South Bend train on a Saturday night was watching the father of some friends of mine. He would give his bindle a throw and then jump off on the run, pick it up and in a hundred feet or so arrive home. He was expected. Rain, snow, hail or heat, he stepped behind two rows of blankets on the clotheslines, took off all his clothes and got into a wash tub full of nearly boiling water and Lysol. His wife proceeded to scrub him from head to toe with a brush. Climbing out, he then put on clean underwear and went into the house to finish dressing while his wife dutifully tossed his dirty clothes, blankets and all into the tub with more Lysol. She didn't fancy his bringing home bedbugs, cockroaches, lice and other unmentionable creatures so she scrubbed him 'till she was practically down to red meat.

The Kennicott house became sort of a free hotel. Friends would come in from Union and stay a few days. My Aunt Alveretta lived there while she taught school at Napavine. My Uncle Jack Guthrie stayed with us for two years while he worked at Dunbar's Hardware Store and later my cousin Doris from New York State lived with us for two years while she attended Chehalis High School. Many a young person lived with us while they also attended the high school since there was often no school in the communities where they lived.

Visiting ministers and their families stayed and even traveling salesmen. One I remember in particular was the Ferry Seed salesman known by everyone as "Uncle Sam." He looked very much like him and did nothing to discourage the idea, even playing up to it a bit. I liked him. He was a happy individual and used to come around about twice a year and stay a few days until he had covered the territory.

And then there was Rosie, the Armenian woman who sold handmade lace. She would always come staggering into our home with two huge suitcases filled with her merchandise. I don't believe she even had a change of clothing because even as a child, I remember the strong aroma of her perspiration. When my mother died, we found drawers and drawers of beautiful handmade lace, some of which Rosie had given her but most which my mother had no use for but purchased from her out of sympathy.

One of our most loveable guests was an old friend of the family from Union, Mrs. Seymore. She used to come about twice a year and stay for a month or six weeks each time. My mother's sight was poor, so Mrs. Seymore did the sewing and mending for us and the hospital. She was always kind to me and I loved her. Many years later when she was ill, she came to the hospital where she stayed until her death. I was twelve or thirteen when my mother came to me and said, "Mrs. Seymore is dying and I can't sit beside her any longer. Would you please come and sit beside her?"

I went into her room and stayed with her, holding her hand and comforting her. She knew she was dying and thanked me for staying with her. As I was holding her hand I saw the color drain from her face and thought she had died, but suddenly a smile came across her face and she said, "Robert, it's beautiful. It's beautiful." And she was gone.

I also had an experience like this many years later when my dear friend Charlie McCutcheon was ill in the St. Helen Hospital. I went up to see him and found his wife coming out of his room sobbing. She told me that Charlie was dying and she just couldn't take it any longer and asked if I would go in and sit with him.

When Charlie saw me he smiled and squeezed my hand and

said, "Thanks. Thank you, Bob." I sat beside his bed saying nothing because there wasn't anything to say. He was too tired to talk but occasionally he would squeeze my hand to let me know he was still there. Then as I watched his face, the color drained out slowly from the hairline to his chest. Suddenly he sat bolt upright, squeezed my hand and said, "It's alright Bob, it's alright." His grasp on my fingers loosened, a long sigh escaped his lips and I knew I had lost a wonderful friend.

When I went out into the lobby and saw his wife sitting there weeping, all I could do was nod my head. She whispered, "Thank you, Bob."

CHAPTER 5

THE WRONG SIDE OF THE TRACKS

As the town of Chehalis moved away from the railroad tracks and toward Market Street, our family began to find ourselves on the wrong side of the tracks. There were three whore houses down on the south end of State Street where the Darigold Store is now. When the madams used to go up town on Saturday afternoons to stimulate trade, they had to pass by our house on the wooden boardwalk. I thought them the most beautiful women I had ever seen! And they smelled so good. I used to wonder why my mother and sister didn't smell that way. You could smell them for ten minutes after they had passed. You could almost see the perfume in the air!

One day when I was on the boardwalk in front of our house peddling my little red automobile, they came by. One of the madams patted my cute little head and gave me a big shining silver dollar! I was so excited that I ran into the house to show my mother the coin. She called it "dirty money." It looked clean to me. "You must give it back immediately as soon as they return," she ordered.

Crestfallen and heartbroken, I went back to wait for them. But when they did come, it was by carriage. They were laughing and waving and feeling no pain as they went merrily on their way and I kept my ill-gotten gain.

I was a very lonely child. I was never allowed to play with the rough boys in the neighborhood. My sister was eleven years older than I, so she was no help—in fact, she was the one who got me in trouble by running to my mother at any misdeed on my part. My mother was strict and punishment severe. I soon learned that God and Santa Claus were always watching over my shoulder and keeping records of my misdeeds, so come Christmas…

I saw and felt little love in my family because although my mother was in the forefront of the doer-of-good-deeds for the church and community, she was autocratic and dictatorial at home. My father for the sake of peace would go along for awhile, but since he had a short temper, I never knew when the explosion would come. It was like sitting on a keg of dynamite. I knew I should love my mother and many nights I would cry myself to sleep because I couldn't.

There was a family of four who lived in a little shack across the street. He was a common laborer and I used to hide in our big hedge and watch when it was time for him to get home from work. The young mother would put on a clean dress and fix her hair, then she would wash the children's faces and freshen them and they would sit on the porch and wait.

The second he showed up down the street they would run to meet him. When they were a few feet away, she would take a few quick steps and jump into his arms. He would then hold her close and give her a long kiss on the lips, then pick up the little girl and throw her on his shoulders. He gave the little boy his lunch pail and held his hand and with his arm around his wife, they walked home to the awaiting supper. I thought it the most beautiful thing I had ever seen. How I wished I belonged to that family and lived in a little shack where there was love instead of my cold fifteen-room house. I often stayed in the hedge and cried.

About the time that I was housebroken I was sent to dancing school. This did a lot for my vocabulary. I learned many new words while trying to express my hatred for the whole idea of being dressed up and forced to dance with a number of homely girls who fouled up an otherwise lovely Saturday afternoon. These classes transpired on the upper floor of the IOOF Hall on Prindle Street.

Not satisfied with screwing up my Saturday afternoons, my parent's threw in Sundays which were a pain in the posterior. After an hour in Sunday school, I had to spend another hour polishing the seat of the family pew during church. I couldn't believe that a kind God would make one suffer so. To further ruin the day, after a big noon meal I was allowed to read or go for a walk all dressed up in my Little Lord Fauntleroy outfit. Other kids were enjoying a ball game or just general hell-raising. It didn't seem fair.

One other means of keeping me out of the Devil's grasp was to see that I was never overstocked with idle moments. Before I was old enough to push the lawnmower by the handles, I was taught I could move it by hooking my right elbow over the handle and by placing my left hand on the wood shaft of the machine, I could make it move. This wasn't easy but if a lot of energy was expended, some grass was cut.

About this time I was judged old enough to milk a cow. The cow and I had several disputes over who was getting the most fun out of the procedure. I couldn't hold the pail between skinny little legs, so I set it on the floor. The cow thought it quite amusing to step into the pail. The use of a pitchfork handle on the base of her tail seemed to discourage this game. Moving on to bigger and better things, she kicked me (milk stool and pail) across the barn. A few swats on the butt with a 1 X 4 plank settled her down and we soon became the best of friends.

Our house and hospital plus the barn, lawn and gardens filled a whole block. We also had half a block to the south of us. On this piece of land stood the wash house, chicken house and yard. This still left enough land for a night pasture for the cow.

At about this time I tried to improve my financial picture. I

34

became salesman for *Saturday Evening Post, Ladies Home Journal* and *Country Gentleman.* You have no idea how it built me up, going up to Mare's Drug Store at 7 a.m. picking up my magazines and going forth to meet the world. Knowing there was practically a captive market just a block and a half from home, I entered the crib house. This two-storied structure had a desk at the front door, but since the desk was not occupied I started down the hall. Over each door was a name; "Lilly," "Pansy," "Rose"... Seeing a light over Rose's door, I figured she was home. I pressed the button. Rose was at home alright, but quite...should I say...*occupied.* She stared at me and told me that I had better get the hell out of there. At that moment the madam appeared and wanted to know what I was doing there. When she understood that I was selling, not buying, she was very kind and said, "Robert, I think you had better contact me at the desk and I'll let you know what magazine we need."

Of course my mother found out somehow about my sale techniques and the crib house was placed off limits. I lost a lot of potential customers.

From the moment I kicked the slats out of my crib, I became an errand boy.

"Here's a dollar. Run up to the market and get five pounds of round steak. Take this nickel and get a loaf of bread. Or a dime and get a dozen doughnuts."

As a recompense for bringing trade to their store I was always given something. From the meat market I got either three or four wieners or a dill pickle from the barrel. The baker always gave me the thirteenth doughnut or a cookie as big as a saucer. I miss those days.

I never should have left kindergarten. While there, in spite of a few slaps, scratches and hair-pulling, I kept my dignity quite well. Thank God they got me out of kindy before my voice changed and I had to shave. Sadly, I was thrown to wolves in the first grade, getting off to a bad start by learning how to fight. It was years before

I discovered that hitting boys in the fist with my nose wasn't the winning move. My nose was one of my most outstanding features; in fact it stood out quite a distance from the rest of my face which should have given me a clue before it was too late. Every boy and half the girls at West Side School could beat me into submission, but do you think for one moment that this bothered me in the least? You know damned well it did. Secretly, I've been a Casper Milquetoast all of my life.

I did, however, have a wonderful first grade teacher, Miss Halpin who made me feel quite at home with the younger set in my class. One day during recess as we were playing games in the grove of fir trees that stood on the school grounds on West Street, one girl took off her fuzzy coat and threw it on the ground. Another girl grabbed my arm and said she wanted to show me something and proceeded to take me over to the coat and pointed out that it was covered with lice. Being a doctor's son, I thought it was my God-given duty to tell the teacher that we were about to be invaded. While we were watching in awe, the girl came over, snatched up the coat from the ground and stalked off, her head held high. I never saw the girl or coat from that day forward.

One bright Sunday morning I walked with my mother to the Presbyterian Church. For some reason we went up Chehalis Avenue, then up Boistfort Street to Market. We were on the corner when one hind wheel of a wagon load of coal broke through the planking. The teamster, yelling and swearing, beat the horses unmercifully but the poor creatures could not pull the wheel out of the hole. A well-dressed drummer (traveling salesman) came across from the hotel, reached up and jerked the driver off the wagon, gave him a couple of hard slaps across the face, made a few remarks about his parentage and said, "I'll help you this time, but if I ever catch you abusing horses like that again I'll kill you. Now get back up there and drive when I tell you to."

The drummer then carefully placed his newly lit cigar on the side-walk, took off his fedora and jacket, laying them beside it, and got behind the obstructed wheel. Reaching down, he grabbed a spoke in both hands and yelling at the driver, lifted mightily. With a crack of the whip the team lunged forward and the wheel rose from the hole.

I never did get much Christianity through my posterior on the hard church pew that day, but this episode taught me a lesson I never forgot.

In the early days Market Street and Chehalis Avenue had been modernized by planking. The planks on Market Street extended from the railroad to St. Helen's Hotel. There you dropped off into bottomless mud. Later, in a bold move toward further moderniza-tion, the brick pavement was put in and the old rotten planks were removed.

When I finally reached the fourth grade, I became the student of a woman who didn't like children, teachers or herself. After sev-eral differences of opinion, I walked out of her class one day and had a quite a tussle with her while I was trying to get my bicycle to go home. At this time I made quite a few remarks about her parent-age. The Principal said that if I made a full confession of my sins on bended knee and asked forgiveness for the bad names I had called her, I might be reinstated into the school system.

My mother, after a consultation with the teacher, came to the conclusion that for once in my life I was right. So I studied at home under my mother's tutelage for the balance of the year. I not only passed the tests for that year, but for the next year also, allowing me to join the sixth grade class the following fall.

I managed to graduate from the West Side School with only a few whippings and entered Chehalis High School. But many of my best friends ended their scholastic career at the end of the eighth grade. This was quite common at that time.

There were several small manufacturing companies in town,

mostly along State Street. At the south end, where the Darigold Feed Store is now, there was a furniture manufacturing plant that put out excellent hardwood furniture of oak, maple, ash and some of the cheaper lines of alder.

At the north end was a wooden pipe manufacturing plant. They made excellent, long-lasting water pipe of concave laminated pieces of fir. The sections were held together by a large collar of wood about eight inches wide, under which the two tapered ends were driven firmly together. The outside was wrapped tightly with wire. The whole thing was thoroughly tarred and then heavily covered with sawdust for easy handling. I know about its lasting ability because forty-years later when some of it was replaced by steel pipes, I used some of the pieces for culverts on my place on Kennicott Hill.

Further down State Street was the Fir Door Factory.

The Carnation Milk Company had their processing plant where Callison's is now and it was Carnation who built the huge smoke stack at Callison's. After pouring the concrete, they kept a slow-burning fire in the center to cure the concrete. After school one day, a friend and I went over to investigate. Above the fire box was an entrance to the inside of the stack. Inside there were rods set in the concrete so up we climbed. The heat and swirling smoke made it uncomfortable and an occasional loose rod sent fear down my spine, but we continued on up. I felt so tall, but the Little Lord Fauntleroy part of me wished I was safely at home. The higher we climbed, the hotter it got so that when I finally reached the top and peeked over the edge to the Chehalis valley below, the wind blew my cap off! Still, I was filled through and through with a glorious sense of achievement.

CHAPTER 6

THE HATFIELDS & McCOYS AND MORE

Lewis County was fortunate in having a fair-sized infusion of mountain folk from Kentucky and West Virginia. They spoke the English of Shakespeare–a speech unsullied by bits of every other tongue in the world which we now call English. These were a friendly, proud and independent people who stood on their own two feet and asked naught of any man.

My history book had a lot to say about the endless feuding of the Hatfields and the McCoys, some of whom settled in the hills of eastern Lewis County. There had been a few shootings and court cases between them, but some of those feuds got trapped and tamed by the marriage bed. During Prohibition these clans prospered. The Hatfields and McCoys mastered the art of fermentation and distillation back in those hills and were able to help out many of the dry, thirsty residents of Lewis County in their hour of need. They made a fine product which they sold at an affordable price. None of their customers went blind, other than getting blind drunk at times. These mountain folk were wonderful friends, but damned mean enemies.

One of the most outstanding families of early eastern Lewis County back then were the Blankenships—hi-spirited, intelligent and fiercely independent, believing that the laws were made for other people. One of Lewis County's most unforgettable sheriffs was a Blankenship. One day while he was driving to the eastern end of the county, he met a nephew who was walking up the road toward him. The sheriff stopped the car and asked him where he was going. The nephew casually explained that he was coming into Chehalis to report to his uncle that he had just killed his brother-in-law.

The mountain folk of eastern Lewis County were often patients in the hospital. They had the custom, as did the early pioneers, of using a ladder to get into the attic which is where most of the family members slept. One day one of the women had come into the hospital for an operation. It had gone well and Dr. Kennicott hoped she could be discharged soon. When my mother came out on the back porch of her home, she saw to her horror, the woman climbing up the back stairs on her hands and knees. "What's wrong?" my mother cried out.

"Nothin' M'am, I just ain't never clumb a ladder like this afore!"

Before leaving those from West Virginia and Kentucky, there are a few families who remain locked in my memory. One was a family of Kentuckians who lived on a poorly-run farm west of Chehalis. Sam was quite a character. He could have doubled for Ichabod Crane. Tall, thin, a bit stooped and leathery, he never had time to run his farm, but was always available for advice whether one wanted it or not.

Sam had a barn that was slowly collapsing. Year after year it got closer to the ground. One hot day about a dozen heifers were under the shade of this half-collapsed structure when I said, "Sam, those heifers are apt to be killed any minute. Why don't you tear the barn down?"

"Robert," he replied, "that there barn's been fallin' down fer years. If they get killed in thar, it's their own damn fault."

Sam's wife was built on the same order as Sam; long, slim, with not much in the way of protuberances. She was a great one to "set and rock." One time when I had gone with my father on a call to a neighbor, I was told to sit and talk with Sam's wife. She was somewhat addicted to an old Southern remedy—the snoos stick. This consists of a small stick, chewed to a pulp on one end. This is dipped into a jar of powdered snuff from time to time and savored and enjoyed until the saliva builds up to the point where expectoration is required. After years of experience this woman could rank among the best in a spitting contest. I was fascinated watching her hit a knothole in the floor with very little splatter.

On this particular day, the window was open and a black cat jumped from the sill to the floor. "Scat!" Mrs. Sam hollered. This, however, had no effect on the cat so without changing rhythm of the rocker; Mrs. Sam shot a stream of tobacco juice right into the face of the cat. There was one screech of agony and the cat was gone.

Another Kentucky family that touched my life was the Williamsons. They lived on a yellow clay hill west of Chehalis. My father was a sucker for all the people without any money, so they were his patients one and all. Dad was making a call and since the weather was hot, I asked a boy about my age for a drink. He led me to their well and lowered the bucket. As I peered down watching the bucket hit the water, I noticed a large sore back salmon swimming around.

"What's going on?" I asked the boy.

He explained that they had caught two in the creek the day before and happened to be having one for lunch and saving the other one for the next day. In spite of the fish, I satisfied my thirst. When we were called in for lunch, here was a whole salmon, head to tail, on a platter. I was given a vast slice plus a half-boiled potato. I had been taught to clean up my plate, so I did. When asked if I would like some puddin', I replied in the affirmative and watched Mrs. Williamson place a large soup plate full of half-ripe evergreen blackberries drowned in skim milk. I shoveled it all down as quickly as possible and got out of the house as fast as I could. Southern hospitality had just about done me in.

41

Mr. Williamson worked at the Wisconsin Timber mill in Littell. Come Saturday night he was wont to go to Chehalis with the boys and spend most of his check on grog. One time his wife got sick of this and went to the paymaster and picked up his check. She had to walk about four miles into Chehalis to cash it. It was miserable, rainy weather so she wore a yellow slicker, black gum boots and a black Sou'wester. When she presented her husband's check to the teller he refused her without identification.

"Call up the paymaster," she told him.

He did exactly that and the paymaster asked him to identify Mrs. Williamson. "Tall and thin and looks like the wrath of God on wheels," came the reply.

"Well?" Mrs. Williamson asked brusquely.

"Thank you kindly. I'll cash your check."

The males of the family all had names that seemed a bit different; Hi, Bi and Si. I think Hi was the father. As soon as Bi was old enough for trouble, he had it–fighting in town and selling moonshine. When I was about ten-years-old I witnessed one such encounter with the law. The police were chasing him and even shot into the air a time or two. I saw him run around behind the building and hide something in the tall grass. When the police caught up with him, they searched him and asked me if I had seen him hide anything. I said I had been so busy watching them shooting their guns that I hadn't seen anything else. After the police left, Bi said, "Thanks, Robert. We'll look in this clump of grass tomorrow." I did and there was a full quart of mountain dew.

There was one girl in town that was quite pretty in a buxom sort of way. Long after her family had escaped my ken, I saw her on the street one day, or rather she saw me. She recognized me and spoke. She was all gussied up and painted and dressed to the hilt and when I asked what brought her to town, she replied that she was living alone in a hotel. When I asked if she was working, she said that she worked in the hotel, that a man had set her up in a room and paid for her food and clothes. She explained that all she had to do was look after the old man's needs and those of his son. When I remonstrated a bit about her mode of life, she said, "It beats the hell out of working in the laundry! Come on up to room 9 anytime, Robert. It won't cost you a damn cent."

I never accepted. Damn.

One family I won't ever forget was the Purcels. Mr. Purcel, or Bert as he was called, always hung loose in his clothes. He was composed mostly of knees, neck and elbows. I always enjoyed watching his Adam's apple pump up and down his neck. Bert played the violin. Although he was allergic to work, he was glad to play the violin for any and all occasions, be it for dance, wedding or funeral. At most occasions there would be food there for him and his family and, if he was lucky, a bit of joy juice on the side.

One night I was asked to stay for supper and Mrs. Purcel said, "You kids go and catch one of them there Plymouth Rock hens and cut her head off, but don't get one what's a-layin'. If you can only get one finger up her, she ain't. Kill her."

The flour sack stood at the end of the work table in the kitchen and when Mrs. Purcel went to get flour for the biscuits she found a hen sitting in the open end of the sack, flapping her wings and squawking. "Well, I'll be darned—looky what she left."

Sure enough, there was an egg in the flour sack.

The last time I ever heard of the Purcels was that one of the boys was teaching music in a school in the eastern part of the state.

When I was a kid I had special privileges at the fire hall since Jimmy Enoch, stepson of the Fire Chief, was a good friend of mine. I was fascinated by the speed and efficiency with which a fire alarm was answered. With the sound of the bell, a cord which kept the three horses in their stalls, dropped to the ground. The horses each went to his position underneath the harness which was hanging from the ceiling with traces connected to the fire engine. The harnesses dropped and collars snapped together beneath—a pull on a cord to open the door, and they were off.

Each day the horses were put through their drill and exercised. With a Dalmatian dog always lying on the engine, they were led down Prindle to State Street and from there down to Main, where they then turned around. Then at the signal they raced up State to West Street, bells clanging and horses lunging. It was a sight to see. As a youngster, this was one bit of daily excitement I rarely missed.

Later when Chehalis got a motorized fire engine, the horses were put to use by the Street Department. That didn't work well, though, because whenever a fire alarm went off, regardless of what they were doing, off the horses would dash to the scene of the fire. Finally they were sold to a farmer far enough from the sound of the bell.

Aside from a few paid firemen, the rest of the force was volunteer, made up mostly of the young punks in town which included me. We got paid two dollars for each fire we fought. When the mill burned down, I fought it from the underside of the dock and I ruined a seven-dollar pair of shoes doing it.

Robert W. Kennicott,
Naturalist 1835-1866

Dr. William Henry Kennicott
1808-1862

Dr. Guy William Kennicott
1859-1944

Harriet Foster Black Kennicott
1863-1942

Early Kennicott home before remodel. Purchased from Dr. J.S. Herndon 1985.

Dr. Kennicott, early Chehalis.

Dr. Guy Kennicott.

Kennicott home after remodel 1903.

Lewis County Hospital, corner of State and Prindle,
1903. Kennicott home in background.

Frances Kennicott 1893-1952

Young Robert's early sales venture with the Frost children, 1909.

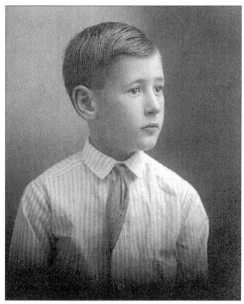

Young Robert, 1911.

Growing up.

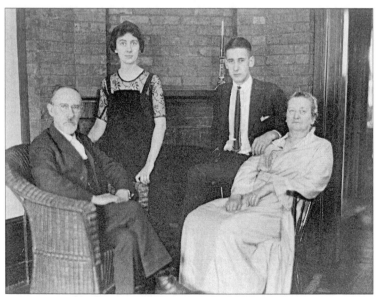

Kennicott family at home in 1919. Guy, Frances, Robert & Harriet.

Robert Kennicott, age 15.

Robert buys property on
Kennicott Hill in 1931.

Young family on Kennicott Hill, 1940.

Early days.

With Grandma Harriet Kennicott, 1940.

Celebrating anniversary with
Florence in her wedding dress.

Florence Day Kennicott, 1940's.

Aunt Frances' house on Kennicott Hill.

53

Dorothy and young Robert with Dad.

Kennicott Ranch, 1963; Julie Pierson, Shannon Simpson, Laurie Pierson.

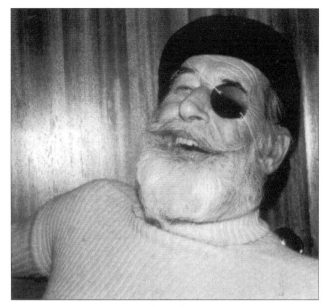

Salty Bob.

Celebrating with me at my college graduation party, 1988.

Good days in Late Afternoon of Life.

Final Days together at the
Care Center celebrating
the Wildest West.

Landmark remains of Kennicott farmhouse, 2012.

Kennicott home (back view) 2012.

The old Russian, George's hand-crafted
"copper still" (distiller) hidden under his
staircase during the Prohibition years.

CHAPTER 7

THE ALLENDERS

The Allenders were important in my early life. Ben Allender and his wife owned and ran a boarding and rooming house on the corner of State and North Streets. The second story was reached by an outdoor stairway. Each room had a door onto the balcony which projected from the building on two sides. This was a working man's eating place and abode.

The breakfast bell rang at six o'clock in the morning as most of the men had to be at work by seven. Food was served family style with platters and serving dishes heaped high with good food. My friend Norman Brunswig used to go there with his parents for Sunday dinner and was impressed with the platters of fried chicken and bowls of mashed potatoes and gravy, all topped off with pies and cakes. The Allenders were good advertisements of the food they served as was their constant companion, a Dalmatian dog.

Naturally with all this preparation and serving of food, there was a lot of garbage. Ben Allender wasn't one to waste anything, so he kept a few pigs in a pen away from the street and down a narrow walk between the G.A.R. (Grand Army of the Republic)* Hall and a small house he owned and rented to a wild Irish family. Quite early every morning, Mr. Allender and his dog took the garbage down to feed the pigs. He was a portly man with a smiling face and happy disposition. You could almost set your watch by his merry whistle with its clear, sharp tone, always in tune. Over the years his repertoire consisted of two rather nostalgic numbers; "The Whistler and His Dog," and "In the Good Old Summertime." Many a morning I awoke to his merry whistle and could tell what the weather was by its sound: clear, overcast or rainy. Each had an effect on the carrying power of the whistle. I'll never forget the morning that the whistle had a soft, velvety sound and I jumped out of bed to a world blanketed in white.

Across from the Allender's boarding house was the village smithy and the home of another Allender family; Sam, his beautiful wife and daughter Olive, who was about my age. Olive was a joy to behold. Everything about her was round—her smiling face, her golden curls, her big blue eyes. She was always immaculate. The blacksmith shop drew me like a magnet and there was a bit of a magnetic pull about Olive too.

Sam Allender was my idea of God. He was very good looking, strong as an ox and the friend of everyone. In my early years the blacksmith shop was off-limits for me and I got my pants dusted every time I was caught down there.

Beneath the back of the smithy's shop was a concrete slab with a hole in the center. This was used to sweat new steel tires on wooden wheels. The tire was laid on the slab and a fire of bits and pieces of wood were laid all the way around it. When the heat had expanded the steel tire sufficiently, the wheel was quickly slipped inside the tire with the hub over the hole in the center of the slab and water thrown on it to quickly shrink the tire onto the wheel and to prevent the wheel from burning.

When the men had finished with the wheel and departed, Olive and I would scrape the bits and pieces of burning wood together on the slab to keep the fire going. Next we would go to Sam's garden and dig into a potato hill and pull out spuds from the size of walnuts on up. Once these were roasting in our fire, Olive went into the house and got salt. We waited until the skins were charred and burnt open and full of ashes. Never in my life have I ever tasted potatoes half as delicious.

Sam must have wondered at times about the small potato crops.

One bright morning I was pulled down the street by some strong power, ending up in Sam's shop. Nobody was in sight, but beside the anvil was a pile of newly-made mule shoes. They were so small and beautifully shaped that I couldn't resist picking one up for closer examination. It almost glowed. I didn't hold it long, however, because the shoe had barely lost its red color and was searingly hot—so hot in fact that when I dropped it, quite a bit of my skin went with it.

Fighting back tears, I raced home. Eyes wide, I attempted to carry on a lively conversation with my mother, standing on one foot, then the other. She asked me if I needed the toilet. I shook my head, "No."

Noticing that my hands were crammed into my pockets, she demanded to examine them. When she saw my seared little paw she insisted on an explanation. Being an instant liar, if not a clever one, I said, "I—I was walking past the blacksmith shop when—someone threw a hot mule shoe out of the door and hit me in the palm of my hand."

My mother said, "Just as soon as I have doctored that hand, we are going right down and tell that blacksmith what I think of men who throw hot mule shoes at little boys." Of course I had to explain that they hadn't exactly thrown it at me, that maybe I had just picked it up. I lied automatically and then caught double hell—first for the naughty thing I did, and again for not telling the truth about it.

One sunny Sunday morning I slipped away with my sling shot and meandered down State Street to Main. At this junction of the two streets, Main became airborne by way of a trestle for both vehicles and foot traffic. I walked out on the trestle watching for rats to shoot at, when I heard a peculiar sound. I glanced down into the mass of evergreen blackberry vines and saw a man lying on his back with his throat cut. He was breathing and blowing bubbles in his own blood.

I screamed and yelled for help, racing toward the Allender's boarding house. There were some men sitting out in front having a smoke after breakfast. They and Sam Allender, the blacksmith, came to see what was wrong.

With his bare hands, Sam tore out a piece of railing and ripped a 12-inch plank from the floor. He dropped this flat onto the berry vines and climbed down onto it, picking up the man and handing him up to the men on the trestle. He tore up another plank and fashioned a stretcher, and they took the man to Dad's hospital. By now I was well ahead of them and had Dad in the surgery when they brought him in. I stayed around and watched him getting his throat sewed up. He lived and in a few days was on his way. Apparently someone had slipped up behind him, slit his throat, gone through his pockets, then pushed him off the trestle and left him to die. They missed his jugular vein. That's all that saved him. It was a good thing I was on that trestle looking for rats that Sunday morning.

CHAPTER 8

BUFFALO BILL COMES TO TOWN

One good thing about living where I did was that the circus unloaded right outside our back gate. One bit of extra noise on the track and I was dressed and out, leaving the family safely asleep in their beds. The elephant car is where I stationed myself with my shirt and pockets filled with windfall apples. I walked up and down the line making the elephants find and get apples out of my clothes. They were very clever at this and we made quite a game of it, much to the delight of the mahout.*

I never had brains enough to be afraid of a strange elephant and never did they give me reason to. When the show was over and they were loading again at night, I was there again with pockets and shirt filled with apples and greeted like a lost friend!

In one circus there was a huge she-elephant who had fallen in love with a Shetland pony. To keep the elephant content while they were being transported, they had built a heavy crib of 2 X 4's in one corner of the elephant car directly in front of the she-elephant. When I was handing out apples, she gave hers to the pony. Then I gave one to her and the pony simultaneously and proceeded on up the line handing out apples to the other elephants. I had one left which I safely hid in the back of my shirt. When I returned to the she elephant, she reached out her trunk to me. I held out my two empty hands and sadly shook my head. Quick as a flash, her trunk went inside my shirt, around the back, grabbing the apple and sticking it in her mouth. Her eyes sparkled! I threw my arms around her trunk and laughed like crazy. Even the mahout chuckled.

All of a sudden it struck me. How amazing that an elephant and two humans, none of which could understand each others' language, could all share the same joke. It was one of life's wonderful moments. The next thing I knew, I was sitting on her back with her holding my foot so I wouldn't fall off. In one swift movement of her trunk she had swept me off my feet and placed me there. And there I sat, the King of the World, until it was time to load the elephants back onto the circus train and leave town.

My father was as big a circus buff as I was. When Buffalo Bill's Wild West Show came to Chehalis, he insisted on taking me to the show in spite of my mother's heated protestations that it was coarse and completely unsuited to my tender sensibilities.

It was a one-tent show, full of action and noise—strictly a cowboy and Indian affair. There were Indian attacks on stagecoaches, trick riding and trick roping and stagecoach races, all dust and action and tumult!

The most thrilling of all was the performance of Buffalo Bill on his beautiful Palomino. He came in at full gallop and swinging under the horse's belly, shot into a shiny metal sheet. At the end of the tent he tossed his empty 30-30 rifle to a man who threw a full rifle back to him. He reversed and came back again at full speed and shot under the horse's belly again. After two or three swipes at full gallop, the metal plate revealed the perfect picture of an Indian's head with two feathers as a headdress—all drawn with bullet holes. I will never forget the thrill.

At the conclusion of the show, Buffalo Bill rode up to a half barrel filled with water, swept off his light colored ten-gallon hat, filled it with water from the tank, gave the horse a drink and then drank from the hat himself. That brought down the house.

When the show was over, Dad took me by the hand and led me into the ring where Buffalo Bill Cody still stood by his horse. My father complemented Bill Cody on the show after introducing himself and me. Bill Cody was a tall leathery person with dark skin and flowing white hair, beard and mustache. What I remember most were his piercing eyes. I don't remember much of the conversation because I was too busy petting his horse's nose. What a big day in the life of a country boy!

CHAPTER 9

GROWING UP FAST BESIDE THE TRACKS

Being the son of a railroad doctor and living beside the tracks meant there was always something going on. I especially loved it when the World War I troop trains came along. I gathered up all the decent apples I could find from our trees and stacked them on the lawn waiting so I could throw them to the soldiers.

But experiences weren't always happy ones. At that time north and southbound trains were allowed to pass each other as they came through town. One day I watched a boy with a bicycle waiting for a southbound train to pass. What he couldn't see was the northbound train coming on the side, but I could. I stood there helpless as he stepped onto the tracks and when he saw the train bearing down on him, he pushed his bicycle out of harms way but he himself froze and was killed.

One evening at dusk I was in the kitchen when I heard movement outside the kitchen door. I opened the door and went out to see two men carrying a stretcher on which was a young woman whose beautiful auburn hair was cascading down almost to the ground. I knew in a second it must be the Callison girl. No one else had hair like that. I knew her well. She used to go horseback riding with Pricilla Gable and my sister. I can't express the feeling of sadness that came over me seeing the body of this beautiful girl whose life had ended.

She had been going down to meet a friend getting off the evening train. The southbound train had just pulled out of the station and she was standing near the tracks with the train rushing past her when she must have lost her balance and fallen against it. It was September 13, 1910 and I was only six years old, but it was not the first time I had seen death.

Accidents weren't always so tragic. One day a drunken hobo came weaving down the tracks with a troop train coming full speed behind him. The engineer saw him and blew his whistle full blast, but the hobo was too drunk to hear it. He was hit just before the road crossing and sailed through the air like a bundle of rags, over the street and the two sidewalks, over the switch and rolled into the ditch. The engineer 'dynamited' the train to a stop. Two soldiers picked up the bundle of rags and brought him to the hospital. Dr. Kennicott examined him and discovered the only injury was a little cut where the engine had crushed the flask which he was carrying on his hip. They put him to bed and when he woke up two hours later all he could say was, "Where's my baul? Where's my baul?" (Usquebaugh-baul: Gaelic for 'perilous whiskey') He had no idea what had happened to him and went merrily on his way.

About this time the Northern Pacific Railroad put in a double track from Seattle to Portland. Living almost beside the tracks, I had a perfect view of the whole operation. There were house cars from the depot to below Main Street. There were three different crews, each with its own cook house. There was one crew of Italians, one of Greeks and one of Sikhs.* These latter fascinated me most. They all wore turbans, long beards, ferocious moustaches, long gowns and were barefooted. One of the Sikhs gave me a patty of some sort with meat between the two pieces of fried bread. It made the tears squirt from my eyes, but left a delightful aftertaste.

When I noticed the water from their water bucket was getting warm and low, I took the bucket over into our yard and washed it and the cup, then filled it with cold, fresh water. I then walked along the line handing out cold drinks to the workers. The boss, a white man, said I was hired as of that moment, and at a man's pay; one dollar a day! When I rushed home to tell my mother of my good fortune, she let me know in no uncertain terms that I was not to go out there on the tracks again—not as a water boy or anything else. Thus ended my short-lived employment.

Thankfully, she didn't cheat me out of some early education. Living beside the railroad tracks guaranteed that. I learned that the Greeks and the Italians would all pee standing. Not the Sikhs. They squatted, holding up their long skirts. There are so many interesting things to learn in the world.

CHAPTER 10

MY FRIENDS

Adjoining the Widow Jones' property to the south of our home was a long, narrow lot. The front was all spaded up for a garden. A narrow boardwalk went clear back to a barn-like structure where Mr. Fauble did cabinet work now and then. Beyond that was a little house where he lived. I was a lonely little bastard and since I had been so much with older people, sought them out as friends. Mr. Fauble was what today we would call a recluse. To me, he was just a lonely soul. He was small and bent. Rheumatism had twisted his body until he couldn't walk without a crutch and cane.

On rainy days, Sunday afternoons or anytime I could escape my mother's eagle eye, I visited Mr. Fauble. One time when I was about ten, he complained that the load of wood he had dumped out back should be piled to dry properly. I told him that I would be glad to do it for him.

He said, "I can't pay you."

"Who in hell asked you to," I replied.

"G.. D… it Robert, don't swear!"

We both enjoyed a good laugh over that.

He never had much to say about his former life or what had crippled him so badly. He kept the conversation on the present or in the future, so I was surprised one day when he told me his son was coming to visit. I said that I was looking forward to meeting him and would he let me know when he was there.

The next time I stopped by Mr. Fauble told me that his son had come and gone. No further comment, which led me to believe that the meeting had not been a very happy one. As time went on, the old man became more feeble and dependent on a wheelchair. He was a lifelong Mason and when it became too difficult for him to make the lodge meetings; they bought him an electric wheelchair.

For years this man sat in his rocking chair, chewed tobacco and spit into a pail of ashes. When he had a fire, he spit against the stove. This added a brown glaze to the stove and a heavy, sweat smell to his house.

I have always suffered from a soft heart as well as head. The thought of anyone not having a big Thanksgiving or Christmas dinner was more that I could bear so on each of those festive occasions, I took a loaded tray of food to my friend. He always said I brought him too much. "Damned near made me sick."

One time when I came home from school I was told that Mr. Fauble had moved on—to what I hoped were greener pastures. No matter how brief the encounter, each of those we meet on the trail either gives something to us or robs us of something. May Mr. Fauble go in peace. We understood each other's loneliness. I remember him saying time and time again, "Robert, this is the shitty end of life." It made little sense to me then, but now having reached that stage myself, it has become my own refrain.

I grew up among adults—mostly women; my mother, sister, nurses, cooks, maid and wash women. My father was the only steady male in my home with the exception of gardeners or stable boys.

Bill Bailey was a man in his sixties; tall, stooped, quiet and unassuming. He had apparently had some culture in his background as he was gentlemanly in his manners and speech. Even though I was only four or five at the time, I would follow him around as he did his chores in the stables. When he had dinner in our kitchen, I always tried to sneak out afterwards and talk with him. I loved him. He was a dear, sweet soul who never had a word of criticism of me, which one could not say of anyone else in my family. When he was in the barn washing the harness and polishing the buckles, I would slip out of my mother's sight and into the barn to be with him. He had a way with horses. They never cut-up when he was around.

I learned a lot of things from him but there was one thing that bothered me. Why did he always act as if life was too much, as if he had been beaten down and unable to cope? I was too young to understand. He lived quietly in his room which was an addition to the nurse's quarters. I knew nothing of his short drunks which caused him to ask my dad to keep his money for him until he asked for it. He needed to save his money. He had a family back East and he wanted to go and visit them, but not until he was sober and well dressed.

One day Bill decided he was ready. He asked my father if he could draw all of his pay. He went to the barber and the men's store. What a transformation! Shave, haircut, new shoes and clothes had made a new man of Bill Bailey. He stood straighter, walked better and really seemed like a different person. He wished us all a tearful goodbye and Dad took him and his new suitcase to the station. They bought his ticket all the way home and after wishing him all the best, my father returned home.

About a week later I heard strange sounds coming from his room and called my dad. He went in with me on his heels. The room stunk of whiskey and of Bill. I could hardly recognize the miserable, whimpering mess on the bed as my friend Bill Bailey. He got one hell of a tongue lashing from my dad.

Apparently Bill had gotten nervous waiting for the train and had stepped over to the *Big Mug* for just one drink. That was the last he knew until they woke him up a week later and kicked him out into the street. He was about the saddest man I think I've ever seen.

He sobered up and carried on as stable boy and gardener. One morning my mother said Bill must have slept in and asked me to go check on him. When I got no answer, I tried the door and since it wasn't locked, I went in. "Mr. Bailey?" I called, but got no answer. I went close and looked at his face and knew that my friend was dead.

Why couldn't I have let him know how much I cared! We had been two lonely people who understood each other. I felt abandoned. I walked around the room in a daze. I had never closely observed his living quarters before. There was a bed and a dresser and a chair, but otherwise the room was stark and bare. Then I stopped and stared. On the wall beside his bed were the little valentines I had given him over the years.

My mother and father saw to it that he had a decent burial. They notified his family back East but never heard from them.

CHAPTER 11

A KALIDESCOPE OF CHARACTERS

THOMAS P. WESTENDORF

"I will take you home again, Kathleen"

Long before Green Hill School for boys and Maple Lane School for girls, the state correctional institution in Chehalis served both boys and girls. In 1891 it was called the *Washington State Reform School* and in 1907 the name was changed to the *Washington State Training School*. Thomas P. Westendorf was the first superintendent and my father was the physician for the school so the two families were well acquainted through the years.

One very vivid memory is when the Westendorfs were at our home for dinner, after which I was sent to bed. Westendorf played the piano beautifully and his daughter, Jennie, played the violin. When the sound of the music drifted up from below, I got out of bed and sat on the steps out of sight. That was the first time I heard the song he had composed, *"I Will Take You Home Again, Kathleen."* The second time was when they both sang and the harmony was so beautiful that just I sat there and bawled.

They were frequent visitors in our home and I was very fond of them. I don't know for sure how much of the song was biographical, but I do know that he wrote it in 1875 and that his wife, Jane, was ill and died here in Chehalis before he was ever able to "take her home." Many years later while visiting in Penzance, England, my wife and I were asked by an Irish tenor to go with him to a pub where he sang. One of his numbers was *"I Will Take You Home Again, Kathleen"* which he introduced as a fine old Irish ballad. He was quite surprised to learn that it originated not in Ireland, but America and that I knew the composer personally and had heard the song when I was a boy.

* * * * *

Hot Tamalaa

Down on Chehalis Avenue, just north of the Crossarm Plant there was a small, miserable little house on stilts above the swamp. Here lived a Turk whose business it was selling chicken hot tamales. Every night he carried his kerosene stove and a basket of tamales and set up business before one or another of the fourteen saloons in town, calling out "Hot tamalaa!" in his high, squeaky voice. This made it convenient for anyone staggering out of the saloon and in need of solid food to stop by and purchase one.

I'll never forget the night when I was a little shaver and my father and I walked up town about eight o'clock. My father, always interested in foreign food, bought two of his hot tamales. We didn't have the beer and wine to go with it, but we stood there on the street and opened up the corn husks and consumed the most delectable viand that ever crossed my pearly teeth! It wasn't until later that I learned from one of my friends who owned a .22 rifle, that he always had a market with the old Turk for anything in the line of meat—be it rabbits, crows, muskrat, cats or rats.

* * * * *

Cohn & Mintzer

Quite early in the 1900's two Jewish men came to Chehalis with a cart made of a couple of buggy wheels with a box about four-feet by six-feet mounted on the axle. Two boards on two sides of the box had a round hole through their extremities, making a handle. It was the same sort of rig that the Mormons used to transport their belongings to Salt Lake.

Cohn was quite an impressive man; not bad looking and quite well built. His partner, Mintzer was a sad sack if you ever saw one. He had an outsized head, huge nose (even larger than mine) and horse teeth. The rest of him wasn't much either. He had a wife who had less hair than any female I ever saw. They moved into a dilapidated church building on Chehalis Avenue just south of Center Street. They pulled their cart up and down the streets and alleys of Chehalis picking up rags, bones, bottles and metal of all kinds. They bought green hides which they salted, also pelts and wool. All of this gave quite an effluvia to their store in which they ate and lived.

One hot summer afternoon when I was about six I hit the jackpot. The hobos cooled their beer in the drip from the Northern Pacific's water tank near our property. I collected the pints and quarts carefully and took them in a sack on my back to Cohn and Mintzer. Quarts were one-cent, pints a half-cent each. One day I struggled with a big load and Mintzer was short three-cents of what he owed me. He said next load he would pay. When I took the next load, he had forgotten about the three cents and later told my father I lied. This had been hard work for me and I was more than annoyed so I proceeded to insult him with language that ought not to be recorded in historical archives.

Many years later Cohn and Mintzer had prospered so greatly that they bought a corner lot on Chehalis and Center. There they built a large brick building and opened a furniture store. They also moved their old church building behind the new structure and continued to buy and sell wool, hides and metal. When the new building was completed and the new stock was in place, they had a grand opening. Above the main floor was the mezzanine which was suspended from the ceiling.

Quite a crowd came to the affair. Many of them went up the stairs to the mezzanine—too many—and it pulled loose from its moorings and fell with its load of furniture and people onto the crowd below. There were quite a number of injuries followed by an equal number of lawsuits. I'm certain that Cohn and Mintzer's misfortune was not the result of my curse.

* * * * *

Old Ole

Around the back fence from the smithy was a sway-backed shanty. The roof had a solid coating of moss four or five inches thick. The windows were always covered and the unpainted board of the house gave it a very dismal appearance. This was the home of Old Ole, a woman of an unknown number of summers with a few bad winters thrown in. Her house faced a short muddy street; ungraded, ungraveled and deeply rutted with no sidewalk leading to her door. In summer a fuel wagon could make it to her front door, but not in the winter.

Once or twice a week she would walk to town to get her groceries, kerosene for her lamps and other necessities usually in liquid form. As she passed by our place I often saw her in her brown heavy skirt, broken shoes and a shawl over her head and shoulders. As I had been raised to be a friendly little bastard, I always greeted her with a "Hello, Ole," to which she replied, "Hello, Robert." That was about as far as our friendship had gotten until one beautiful summer evening.

75

I had gone out to retrieve my tools from where I had been trimming the hedge, when I heard a pitiful moaning in the long grass just outside our yard. I jumped the hedge and went to investigate. Poor Ole had a skin full of gin and had fallen in the long grass and couldn't get up. I helped her to her feet and she gathered up her bottle and groceries and the two of us lurched over the rough road to her door. She was a pitiful looking old woman but my mother said she had been a beautiful young girl when she first knew her.

The wages of sin must have been below union scale.

* * * * *

The Whelans

About 1914 when I was ten years old, Kenneth Whelan and his parents moved into the pink house next to the G.A.R. Hall. One day this lad came walking down the street barefooted in the dust of State Street. He said, "We've just moved in and I'd like to have you meet my maw and paw."

I went with him to his home. His father was a long, lank, lean Kentuckian. His mother was a vision of loveliness. She had a very compact little figure and blue eyes you could drown in. When she met me she said, "Robert, I'd like you to be a friend of Kenneth."

I said, "That's fine. We don't hate each other."

After that whenever I could sneak away from home, I went over to their house because I felt welcomed there and a part of the family. I used to look at Ken's mother and wonder why I hadn't been blessed with a mother like that. One time when I was over there I learned a lot more about them. Ken told me about his early life, living in a camp wagon and following the sheep over the hills of Montana. His father was a sheep herder.

They told me a story that made me cry myself to sleep at night.

After herding another man's sheep for years, he had taken his pay in sheep. They had put the sheep in stock cars and headed up into the government forests. They stopped the train at the edge of the government forest, opened the doors to the cars and urged the sheep to jump out. Two of them broke their legs but the rest moved up into the pasture above the track. There was a beautiful flower growing profusely on the mountainside and the sheep, being starved, ate everything in sight. It wasn't long before they bloated and died. He lost nine-tenths of his flock.

After that he gave up and moved west, bringing his beautiful wife and son. I don't know what work he did to support his family, but his wife and Ken lived near us for a little over a year. The sequel to this story is that one night the phone rang and the soft Kentucky voice of Mr. Whelan said that they were in a bit of trouble and would my father come out as soon as possible. They had moved to a hardscrabble ranch on the top of a hill in the country. He said that he would meet us at the main road with a lantern and he would take us the rest of the way.

We saw the lantern at the side of the road and there was Mr. Whelan waiting with his crude sled made from vine maple with upturned ends for runners and planks crosswise for the bed. Once we got aboard, he picked up the reins, slapped the horses in the butt and we took off. "You all best set low so we don't tip over," he said as we moved through the mud and rocks toward the cabin.

I grabbed my dad's bags and followed him into the cabin. It was poorly lighted by one or two kerosene lamps and as hot as the inside of an oven. Mrs. Whelan was lying on a double bed in the one-room cabin. Beside the bed was a midwife who said she had worked all afternoon trying to "get the kid out of that girl, but she sure-nuff didn't make it."

My father opened a can of chloroform. He handed me a cone, punctured the can and told me, "Drip a few drops on the cone, hold it over her nose and mouth until I tell you to stop." When she was completely relaxed he reached into her with a two-pieced instrument which he fitted around the head of the fetus. The head came out, but that was all. My father used his greatest swear word "damnation!" then proceeded to put on a rubber glove greased with Vaseline and reach in, removing the rest of the fetus bit by bit. The room and the smell just about did me in.

My father turned to the midwife. "What brought this about?"

"I tol' her to reach up there with a lead pencil and puncture its head."

My dad exploded in anger with words worse than damnation. "If I ever hear of you giving advice to or touching another woman you'll spend the rest of your miserable damned life in the penitentiary! Now, get out and don't ever come back!"

The woman left without another word.

I looked around and noticed my friend Ken wasn't anywhere in sight. "Where is he?" I asked his paw.

"He's out a'walkin' the hills," Mr. Whalen said sadly.

I never saw them again.

* * * * *

Classmates, Gin and Cow Manure

In the eighth grade I remember an incident in school when the girl sitting ahead of me put her head on the desk and promptly began snoring. The teacher called on her and she didn't raise her head. The teacher came back and shook her shoulder, but was unable to arouse her. "This girl is sick," she said.

"No," I replied, "she is drunk."

"What do you mean, drunk?"

"Can't you smell the gin?" I asked.

She lifted the girl's head. The rouge and mascara had run and her face was a mess as well as her long black curls.

The teacher got quite excited. "This girl is definitely sick."

When I mentioned the fact that her father pimped for her, her older sister and her mother, that this was Monday morning and that she had had a rough weekend, the teacher couldn't believe me. She called the Principal down and with my help, walked her out into the hall where they threw cold water on her face from the drinking fountain. This partially revived her. The Principal asked me about my knowledge of the situation and I told him that she lived two blocks down the street from me and repeated the sad story.

Some action must have been taken because I never saw her or the family again.

Another interesting classmate was a girl who lived on a small dairy farm on the edge of town. Her name was Leah Zastrau. She was tall, bony and thin and wore high shoes all broken out and twisted which came up to the calf of her leg. Her hair was thin, scraggly and nondescript—her face, bony and angular. She had a big nose, deep lackluster eyes and wore one dress all year long. The dress was so badly faded you couldn't tell the color. Leah had a strong aroma of cow barn as she had to do the milking before school. We made unkind remarks about her odor and the cow manure on her ungainly shoes but she took our insults without umbrage.

Back in those days we had a lot of spelling bees, vocabulary and mathematics contests. Along about seventh or eighth grade, this girl put all to shame with her ability to add long columns of figures and do rapid multiplication or division. We had inter-school competitions where the teachers read off four digit numbers as many as twenty at a time. The students in competition would then write them on the blackboard, competing for the correct answer. When the last number was read, Leah would draw the line and immediately write the correct answer because she had already totaled the numbers as she wrote them down. Then she would go back from the bottom of the column to the top as a second check, but she was seldom wrong the first time. No one around could compete with Leah Zastrau. I never heard of her after that. I don't know if anything was ever done to capitalize on her unusual talent. She probably married a little dairy farmer and had cow manure on her hands the rest of her life.

* * * * *

Thumb or Not So Thumb

One day a Swede came in to the hospital. He had cut off his thumb the day before with a sharp axe. The man attempted to put it back in place, wrapping it up with his bandana handkerchief, but because it hurt so much, he went to the nearest saloon instead of the doctor to find relief. The Swede got gloriously drunk, then passed out which is why he didn't get to Dr. Kennicott until the next day.

"Doc, I tink you best look to my thumb. I cut him off yesterday. Maybe you best sew it back on."

Taking off the blood-soaked bandana, my father realized the thumb had already started to grow back. "But you have put it on backwards. If I take it off, straighten it up and sew it back, it may not grow again. Can you get along with it in this position?"

The Swede said "Ya, ain't too bad. Let 'er be."

And he spent the rest of his life with the thumb nail pointing toward the palm of the hand.

CHAPTER 12

WOBBLIES AND MORE

The city block bounded by the railroad, Center, State and North Streets has seen a lot of history. The Presbyterian Church had been on State Street near our house. When the church moved, my family bought the building and moved it onto this block of land. When the West Side School burned down in about 1910, this old Presbyterian Church building was used for the school. Later the building was torn down and two residences were constructed of the material. Some of the land was once the site of the Lewis County Courthouse and jail and the soil was still full of the bricks that had been part of the jail. After the Courthouse was moved to the Great Western Hotel across the tracks, we used the lot for our cow pasture. One day in 1916 when I was just twelve years old, a troupe train stopped near our home and an army officer jumped out. As I was standing there he asked me if I knew who owned that block.

"Yes, my father does," I told him.

I took the officer to the hospital where Dad was working at the time. He was the Commanding Officer for the Yakima National Guard Company E which had just come up from Calexico, where they had been guarding the border against the inroads of Pancho Villa. He wanted permission to make camp on this open block of land next to the railroad as they had been sent here to guard the bridges against destruction by the IWW.* Members of the IWW (Industrial Workers of the World), were known as the "Wobblies." In 1919 they were involved in what became known as the "Centralia massacre."

Dr. Kennicott gave his permission and pledged full cooperation. This brought about one of the most pleasant and exciting experiences of my young life. We had been using this bit of land for night pasture for our cow. Watching the speed and efficiency of Company E in transforming this cow pasture into a neat army camp was fascinating. In what seemed like minutes, the cow patties were gathered into a pile and buried, an outhouse dug and a row of neat little tents set up.

I have never felt more proud and important. I was allowed freedom to come and go in the camp as I wished, though no one else was allowed there. My particular friend was a Sergeant with a marvelous head of red hair and moustache.

Of course all this called for a flag pole. My father and I went up the hill for a suitable tree. What I chose was the most miserable specimen on the hill. It had enough limbs for two trees and was crooked besides. It was big and gnarly and by the time we were halfway home, I wished we had left it on the hill. Scraping the bark off revealed its deficiencies even more. Nevertheless, we painted it white and on the top my father put a gilded toilet bowl float! Suddenly I wasn't feeling so proud and important anymore. Humiliated, I got out of there as fast as I could.

Later I realized that was a big mistake because when I came back I learned that most all of Company E had come over and with great pomp and ceremony had raised the flag pole and the flag. *Without me*. After the raising of the flag, Company E moved to their permanent headquarters to the concrete building on the corner of State and West Street.

I meandered over to the deserted campground and fooled around with the fire they had left after policing the ground. Dejected, I lingered there until dark, then walked home where a birthday party was in full swing. Thanks to the gilded toilet bowl float flagpole disaster, I had completely forgotten it was my birthday.

Decoration Day is the once-a-year day when everyone in Chehalis decorated graves. One such day stands out clearly in my mind, for no particular reason. It must have been an exceptionally dry year because I wore nothing but bib overalls. It was warm and the dust in the street felt good between my toes. As ten o'clock approached, more and more women came to our house to see if they couldn't "borrow some flowers." They stripped our yard of lilacs, both lavender and white, oriental poppies, roses, lily of the valley and maidenhair ferns. Also any tulips, narcissus or daffodils that still hung on.

When every flower in the valley had been obtained, made into wreaths or groupings, the people piled into wagons, carriages and a few cars owned by the villagers and took off to the cemetery to distribute their gifts of memory. I felt left out because I didn't have any relatives in the cemetery.

I was quite impressed by my many elderly friends all dressed up in blue or gray and wearing ribbons and medals. Most of them used canes or a crutch. One man had one sleeve pinned up almost to his shoulder which told me he had lost an arm in the war. After a service at the cemetery, they came back to the G.A.R. Hall and had a day of eating and renewing old friendships. At the cemetery they took away the sad bleached little flags of yesteryear and in their place set new flags to stand against the sun and storm for another year.

It pained me to see fewer and fewer of my old friends come to meet at the Hall. It wasn't long before no one came and the hall was torn down. What I will never forget is that just before ten o'clock that day a few big drops of rain fell from a black cloud. The smell of those drops on the dust was wonderful. No scent in the most cherished perfume can compare to it.

One of the most amusing things that happened in our town

was the funeral of a bartender whose name I can't even remember. I doubt that he had ever been inside a church in his entire life. But his wife and daughter, being good Presbyterians, had to see that his passing out of this world was duly recorded and in the Christian manner.

There was a pretty good turnout for his funeral; mostly friends of his daughter, but also a few of his old customers. It was quite a decorous affair up until the conclusion of the service, at which time the minister announced that the organist would now play one of the deceased's favorite pieces; "*Crossing the Bar.*" During this rendition, his friends could come forward, pass the coffin and continue out the side door. There were several moments of very strange silence and there were smiles on the faces of all those who gazed upon the face of the Dear Departed.

CHAPTER 13

GRANDMA BORST GETS A NEW HIP
AND OTHER WONDERS OF THE WORLD

My father was very inventive as a surgeon. His medical genius lay in bone surgery. It was said that the professional error of his career was in not having remained in the medical center of Chicago where he could have specialized and where his miraculous innovations could have been observed by the world of medicine. He was always looking for a better way to do things.

One day Grandma Borst was brought in to the hospital with a broken hip. He studied her condition and explained her options. "The accepted practice in a case like this is to put you in a cast from heel to armpit. This keeps the person immobile so that within two weeks time the patient usually dies of pneumonia. Now, I would like to try something new. If it doesn't work, we can always fall back on the accepted practice." Grandma Borst and the family gave him permission to go ahead.

What he had in mind was to open the hip joint and nail the two ends of the bone together. For this he needed a silver nail. He tried but could not get the piece he wanted so instead, sent me up to the hardware store to get galvanized finishing nails of various sizes. He opened the periosteum, drilled holes from the shaft to the head of the bone and drove in the nails, being careful to countersink the head of the nails. He drew the periosteum back into place, sewed up the wound leaving room for drainage. Surprisingly there was very little and the wound healed. The accepted medical idea at that time was that once the liquid was drained from a joint, it would never replace itself. He proved this to be false. The operation was successful and Grandma Borst was able to walk again with the help of a cane.

Strangely enough, two other older women came in with broken hips that year and he repeated the operation with the same success. About two years later, I read in one of his medical journals that a famous Parisian doctor had performed virtually the same operation and his patient was able to sit up in a wheelchair. All three of my father's patients were walking and one who had previously used a cane now used one crutch.

I asked my father why he hadn't reported his success to medical journals.

"It's unethical to advertise," he replied.

Spring was a time to be dreaded. My father always came out of the winter hibernation with more energy than good sense. He had a man and team come in and plow up the quarter of an acre south of our house behind the hospital. After that there was a lot of pressure put on me to finish spading the garden. The first warm day of spring got into my father's blood and I remember that on this particular year we planted a huge garden about one month too early. The weeds sprang up while our seeds rotted. About a month later I was encouraged to cut the weeds and replant the seeds. One year we had seven varieties of tomatoes, none of them very good. Salsify, otherwise known as "Oyster Plant," was a must. One dish of soup made from this plant with Dad's "oohing" and "ahhing" about how good it was took care of things. The rest of the row went to seed–until next year.

Some appreciated his talents in gardening, however. Mr. Leonard Sourdes of Chehalis loved to talk of his ability in plant experimentation. Plant grafting fascinated him. He had an apple tree with three or four different kinds of apples growing from the one tree. He also had grafts of four different plums growing on the one wild plum tree. There was also a hedgehog cactus which sprouted five or six different kinds of cactus. The similarity in plant and human growth fascinated him.

On the extreme north end of Pennsylvania Avenue was one of the wonders of the world. The two-storied white house, the barns and several chicken houses formed three sides of an open barnyard in the center of which was a colossal pile of junk. It contained rusty milk cans, rolls of barbed wire, tin cans, bottles and more. On the top of the pile was a broken pitcher pump attached to about twenty feet of rusty pipe. The pipe stuck out over the driveway high enough for a load of hay to pass under it without difficulty.

I had heard about the pump and pipe from my father. Gazing upon this piece of useless equipment was a constant pleasure to me, but not to Dad. One night, hurrying back from a late call, his team stopped short and wouldn't move. Dad found the road blocked by Cogswell's team and wagon; team and driver asleep with the pump and pipe sticking out the back.

Mrs. Cogswell, who probably wasn't responsible for this mess, was rather short and stocky with a figure like a sack of grain with a string tied around the middle. She wore thick lens glasses which made her eyes look like two boiled gooseberries. She was a terrific worker and kept several chicken houses full of White Leghorns, selling her eggs to all and sundry.

Mr. Cogswell was thin and scraggly. He bent backward from the waist with his arms and hands forward and elbows back. His face was craggy with a prominent adams-apple capable of a slide trombone effect. Truth be known, he looked like a poorly constructed scarecrow.

When I was about ten-years-old I was handed over to the tender loving care of a cow—or was it the other way around? I took Bossy to pasture in the morning and home at night. I shoved great quantities of provender in the front end and took away what seemed like greater quantities from behind. How she managed this I'll never know. Whenever she became somewhat restive, she stepped on my feet, stepped into the pail of milk, or kicked me across the barn. One day I told my father that she was showing more and more displeasure with life and had lost any love for me that she once had. He knew exactly what to do. He gave me a dollar and told me to take Bossy to Mr. Cogswell. She had been there before. Talk about the memory of elephants. My cow beat those elephants a mile. I didn't have to lead her; in fact I was airborne most of the way with my feet touching terra firma only from time to time.

Mr. Cogswell escorted us both to the barn. There the cow was put into a stanchion and the bull brought in and introduced. He was somewhat restrained by a rope that was snapped into the ring in his nose. After a bit of sniffing about, he rose to mount, whereupon Mr. Cogswell grabbed the shiny rod and directed it to home base. When I asked about this procedure I was thusly instructed, "Robert, me and you was built different from a bull. He has a pecker that is made of gristle. If he was to miss on his lunge and break his prick, he ain't worth a damn except for hamburger or sausage."

With all of this valuable knowledge packed away in my little head, I took the cow and started home. About every fifty feet she would whirl around as if she had left something behind and we each tried to show our superiority over the other. This was quite hilarious for the girls along the street who made various remarks, leading me to believe that their knowledge of the world even surpassed mine.

Mr. Cogswell's cattle were Red Polls, a dual purpose animal which meant they weren't worth a damn for either milk or beef. They are a bit light for beef and the cows produce a light blue liquid which makes today's 2 per-cent milk look like solid food. Mr. Cogswell took his cattle to all the fairs around and had a bushel of ribbons for his efforts. No one else owned or would own such a useless breed, so he won against no competition.

Mr. Cogswell had a team of black horses that were built very much as he was; sway-backed and ribby with long, thin necks. The last time I ever saw him was up on Market Street in front of Waltar's Market. There he sat, a vision of Ichabod Crane on his black mare with about twenty feet of rope wound round her neck. He was sitting in a deep depression in the middle of her back, a basket of eggs on each arm. He called out and Beans Waltar came out and relieved him of his burden. Mr. Cogswell waited on his steed with great dignity while Beans counted the eggs, filled one basket with his grocery order and brought it out with his change.

Cogswell then turned the mare around and moseyed down the middle of the main street toward home. The West was full of characters and Mr. Cogswell was definitely one of them.

In his earlier years Mr. Cogswell had been married to the sister of Mr. Millet, one of Chehalis' distinguished citizens. When his first wife died, Mr. Cogswell, always frugal, dug his own wife's grave. Someone told of seeing him that day, eating his noon-day snack, sitting on the edge with his feet dangling in his wife's grave.

Mr. Millet was a founder of the Coffman-Dobson Bank and the law firm now known as Armstrong and Vander Stoep. It was he who gave the baseball field on Chehalis Avenue to the city. Mrs. Millet was a member of the Childs family who owned the chain of fine restaurants in the East. But the real character of people often shows up in the little things they do. As long as Mr. Cogswell lived, the Millets and their daughter, Annie Gray Frost, never forgot him. Whenever they visited Chehalis from their home in California, they always saved time for a visit with Mr. Cogswell.

CHAPTER 14

THE FLU EPIDEMIC OF 1918

During the terrible flu epidemic of 1918, Chehalis and Lewis County were not spared. Here as everywhere else, people were dying en masse. My father, as well as all doctors, were going out on calls day and night. By this time, we had a Willys four-cylinder Overland and even though I was only fourteen-years-old, I found myself the driver for my dad on most of these calls. The car had no heater and Dad wrapped himself in a huge imitation buffalo rug. By keeping warm in this manner he could sleep as I drove from one call to the other. When he went in on a call, I would bundle myself up in the buffalo rug and sleep until he would come out. This lasted for about a week until I caught the disease myself, at which time he had to do the driving himself. By this time my mother had it too. Still, in spite of looking after us, he continued on reaching out to everyone in need. His success rate was amazing—he lost only two patients. These he lost because—according to him—they did not follow his instructions.

One was a Greek who was in the hospital. His orders were that he must be kept completely quiet. Still, the relatives kept coming around. They called in the priests who came in to give him the last rites. During this process, the patient had to sit up for the blessing, and with all the emotional and physical stress, it was too much for him. All this happened without informing my father. It was too late when my father got word of his death.

On one call he made while I was driving, he went into the bedroom and discovered they had closed the window when he had ordered it be kept open for fresh air. With all the pressure and overwork and loss of sleep, my dad's patience had been worn thin. He picked up a chair and threw it through the window.

I had been sitting in the car waiting for Dad when the chair came flying out. I never knew what happened except that this terrible scourge had affected all of us in a way that would be etched on our memories forever.

Later on, Dr. Kennicott reminisces; *"And the young doctor of yesteryear, so full of energy and hope. Well, he too has disappeared. Gone with his old horse, his old saddle bags, his nasty messes and his smelly clothes. Yes, got so stiff he couldn't ride any more and quit. A good old fellow in his day, God bless him. More than just a doctor, friend, a consultant in times of stress. His was the hand gentle and kind that ushered them into this strange complexity we call life. His the hand that banished the ills of their growing years. And when the shadows were falling and the lamp of life fluttered and expired, his the hand, gentle as a mother's, that soothed the pain-wracked frame, and closed the tired, frightened eyes. His kindly face, the first to greet them on their forced arrival, and the last they looked upon ere they began their journey into the mysterious beyond.* (Read before the monthly meeting of Lewis County Medical Society, Centralia, WA Dec. 9, 1929)

CHAPTER 15

PUBERTY, JOY JUICE AND
THE FACTS OF LIFE

When I was fourteen-years-old, due to the fact that my father was a doctor and my mother was a Presbyterian, I got my first real job. George Sears hired me at one dollar per day seven days a week to do odd jobs in his drug store. My hours were from seven a.m. to six p.m. with one hour off for lunch. My chores were not excessive. All I had to do was arrive a bit before seven a.m. and the moment the front door was open, rush to the soda fountain, grab an old baseball bat and pack the ice around the three tubs of ice cream; vanilla, chocolate and strawberry. Next, I broke out the hose and washed the sidewalks and windows on two streets; Boistfort and Pacific Avenues. After that I took a push broom and did the entire floor space of the store. Last came dusting which took up the major portion of the morning.

After Mr. Sears, the second-in-command at the store was a big Frenchman who was a druggist named Alfonso, commonly know as "Fons." He had one eye looking down the street and the other toward the Widow Jones'. He really had a lot to do with getting me safely through puberty.

One day he said, "Rush this order up to the Palm Rooms." I took off and after climbing about twenty-five steps, arrived at a closed door and a push button. I rang the bell and almost immediately the door opened, and to my wondering eyes, who should appear but a prostitute, loosely draped in a very sheer housecoat and nothing else. I handed her the package and said, "You owe me two dollars and fifteen cents."

She said, "Can't we trade this out?"

I replied that this was a business deal, cash not tail, pay up or go to hell.

I grabbed the money and left hurriedly.

When I arrived back at the store Fons said there had been a complaint by one of their best customers and that I had insulted her and would have to go back and apologize.

Knowing him quite well by that time I said, "You dirty …….. you set me up." He laughed like crazy and we were the best of friends from then on.

When not otherwise occupied, I was supposed to tackle the boxes and barrels of dirty bottles in the basement. As I pulled the last barrel out of the corner, I heard a bottle hit the concrete floor. When I looked to see what had happened, there stood a full quart of "Old Sunnybrook," cracked and leaking slowly. I held the two halves of the bottle together to the best of my ability and ran up the stairs calling to Fons to get a funnel, a beaker and a filter paper. We salvaged almost the entire amount, and this took the place of afternoon tea for the two of us.

George Sears, the owner of the store was a model of propriety and a pillar of the Presbyterian Church. If he'd had any idea of what was going on in his store he would have croaked.

Later I found a two-quart bottle of grain alcohol. Fons tested it and found it good. If things were quiet in the late afternoon, I would take about four ounces of the alky over to the soda fountain and build two tall drinks with fruit syrup and soda water. We were feeling a bit silly from our drinks one afternoon when a well-dressed woman came into the store and asked for some toilet paper. Fons went into a speal about the three grades that we carried; "the plush finish, the ordinary and the sandpaper finish, guaranteed to take off all of the new and part of the old."

I panicked and ran out the back door. Later Fons laughed and told me that she was a Madam and an old friend of his. Every young boy should learn the facts of life by working in a drug store.

Later in life as I began to take up some of the burden of support, I could see my mother and father going deeper and deeper into debt while continuing their extravagant ways. I wanted to give up and go off on my own, but I couldn't. When I would explode to a good friend, Gussie Coffman, she would calm me down, pointing out all the good they had done for so many people. I couldn't leave them, so I would go back and put up with it for one more week. And another. Then my father broke his hip and that settled it. Only my sister and I were able to prevent their going into bankruptcy.

I must mention two remarkable women who had a great influence on me in my formative years.

The first aforementioned was Gussie Coffman. She was the wife of Harry Coffman, the founder of Coffman Insurance Company. She was a close friend of my mother's; a beautiful, elegant and refined lady, with a deep understanding and appreciation of others. She seemed to understand the loneliness and frustrations of my childhood. She was my safety valve. I could always tell her my troubles and she could somehow smooth things out.

One day Gussie said to me, "Robert, you are the kind of person who can sit on the curb on a rainy day with the mud running down the gutter and see the rainbow colors made by a splash of oil."

I told her she was wrong. I not only saw the mud, *I got into it.*

"Well," she replied, "it washes off."

The second remarkable woman was Anna Koontz, a person who

did more to promote the culture of our community than any other single person. She was the granddaughter of Matilda Koontz Jackson, wife of John R. Jackson of Jackson Court House fame. But more important, she was *the* Librarian for Chehalis for many, many years. She had a rich knowledge of good literature and by her deep appreciation taught others to love and appreciate our literary heritage. Her most unique quality was her understanding of people. Because of this, she was able to match the literature with the individual.

As she did for other young people in the community, she directed my reading. For many years even while I was still in the West Side Elementary School, she would introduce me to Dickens, Ibsen, Tolstoy, Thackery and many others. "Now Robert, to understand these writings, you must first know about the author. His works will mean so much more to you when you know the man."

She was right. I read everything about Tolstoy, and then his books one after the other until I was so immersed in his works I could almost feel it, as though I were there; the cold Russian winters, the treatment of the serfs, how the people would go almost insane with the coming of warm weather.

I devoured Kipling at home and in the library. I read Galsworthy from beginning to end. Dickens I couldn't like, the world was too hard. I can still hear Miss Koontz when I entered the library; "Oh, Robert, here is a book you will love!"

Anna Koontz was a little woman, quiet and self effacing. Perhaps being a librarian for so long influenced her soft speech, almost a whisper. She was a valued member in the community, including the St. Helen's Club and they benefitted greatly from her cultural background.

She had a most deliciously impish sense of humor which she seldom would allow others to see. When the St. Helen's Club put on a play many years ago, Anna Koontz played the butler. It was a minor part and she had very few lines but the power was her presence and her pantomime. She was so hilarious in a most serious way that it almost stopped the show. The audience was in hysterics whenever she made an entrance. They saw an Anna Koontz they had never seen before.

To this quiet little person, Chehalis owes a debt deeper and more lasting than to the businessmen and politicians who usually commanded the limelight.

* * * * *

There were so many quiet, unassuming people who made their mark and to whom all of Lewis County owes a deep and lasting debt of thanks. Not every hero found honor, nor every lost soul recognition—but every restless soul who walked along the brick or boardwalk streets and paths of our memory became part of our heritage. Their flower of youth is gone, but they remain etched in our own hearts and drive us on toward our dreams.

I SHALL BE SATISFIED
By
Guy William Kennicott 1899

I shall be satisfied, but, oh—my restless soul, not yet.
Not while the morning gleam lights up the sky
Not while the blood runs warm and life is high
Not while the flower of youth with dew are wet
I shall be satisfied, but, oh—my restless soul, not yet.

I shall be satisfied, but, oh—not yet my restless soul, not yet
Not yet, 'tis noontide and the sun's hot beam
Fills the hot world and slows the rushing stream
A thousand duties press and must be met

I shall be satisfied, but oh—my restless soul, not yet.

I shall be satisfied, but oh—not yet my restless soul, not yet
Not 'till the life grows dim, the pulses slow
Not 'till the heart grown tired and life is low
Not 'till the night has come, the sun is set
I shall be satisfied, but oh—not yet my restless soul, not yet.

On December 27, 1990, Robert W. Kennicott died at the age of 86. His beloved wife, Florence lived to be 106. The words of his father's poem might have come from young Robert's own pen and life, especially as the years passed and the sun began to set.

Not yet, my restless soul, not yet....

AFTERWORD

Guy William Kennicott, born in Chicago on January 29th, 1859, died on March 13th, 1944 at the age of 85. Having come to Chehalis in 1895, Dr. Kennicott was known as one of the last of the "horse and buggy doctors." He built and operated the first hospital in the county located at the corner of State and Prindle Streets. It is said that he never refused to answer a call, regardless of weather and distance. Dr. Kennicott himself came from a family of pioneer doctors. His father, Dr. William Henry Kennicott, a dentist, and his brother, John, were among the first medical providers in Chicago, just as the name was changed from Fort Dearborn. Guy Kennicott's wife, Harriet Foster Black Kennicott, born in 1863 in West Hebron New York, died on March 22, 1942, two years before the doctor's passing. Besides teaching school, she was active in the hospital, the community and in affairs of the Presbyterian Church. Guy and Harriet Kennicott had a daughter, Frances Caroline Kennicott, in addition to their son, Robert, both now deceased. Their two grandchildren are, Dorothy Martinez-Kennicott of Mountain View, California and Robert Day Kennicott of Bainbridge Island, Washington.

Robert William Kennicott, the author of this memoir was born in Chehalis on April 12, 1904 and grew up in the Kennicott family home on State Street. He married Florence Day in September 1935. They met while Florence was teaching school in Centralia. Bob was dating a friend of Florence's, MaryLee, while Florence was dating Bob's friend, Norman Brunswig who later owned the shoe store in Chehalis. MaryLee ended up marrying Norman and Bob married Florence.

Bob says, "Florence and I never went out together before marriage because I couldn't afford to take her out, and also because I figured postage was cheaper than nights on the town. Florence has a Master's degree in English and Drama. As for me, after being kicked out of five schools of higher learning, I have only a B.S. degree in any subject you care to mention and some you don't."

"During the years of the Depression before I met Florence, I had gathered up all my sheckles, borrowed all I could from friends (having very few) and made a down-payment on a worn out, miserable piece of land on the top of a red clay hill known today as Kennicott Hill. This property consisted of one-hundred and twenty acres, about ten acres of which were cleared. The rest was covered with large stumps and brush and a wee bit of standing timber. My entire purchase included two houses, three barns, five wells (most would go dry in summer) and a team of horses, plow, disc, harrow, hay rake, mowing machine, hay wagon, a three-man drag saw and a two-horsepower engine. For all of this I paid the handsome price of twenty-five-hundred dollars. I gradually acquired 587 acres in all, raising hogs, sheep and cattle."

Bob's life remained full and the hogs, sheep and cattle should have kept him out of trouble but it didn't. His uncommon childhood and adolescence probably set him up for more than his share of dubious escapades. Soon after he purchased the Kennicott property, he met George,* a scrappy White Russian* peasant living on an adjoining 40-acre piece of land.

These were the days of Prohibition and George had managed to hide a magnificent copper "still" in a boxed-in staircase which set them up for many a wild Russian dance (not Swan Lake). "The foot-deep accumulation of prune pits and apple cores on the floor of the kitchen of the cabin made me realize quite a bit of cooking had gone on there." Robert could not have been more delighted. This worked quite well until a wife and children threw in a few complications, but AA eventually managed to settle the matter and Robert—staying clean and sober (intermittently) after that—moved on to raising the family, hogs, sheep and cattle and "burning an ungodly amount of stumps" day after day, year after year.

The children became fond of George but not his culinary skills. Dorothy and young Robert remember his shot-filled crow borscht made with home-grown beets, cabbage and onions and topped off with Eagle Brand condensed milk instead of sour cream.

"In the Kennicott farm house was a kitchen stove, the old type with a reservoir beside the oven. The reservoir was cracked and unusable. The fire-box was also cracked so that flames shot out into the oven and broke all the wedding Pyrex. The front two legs were gone but the stove was somewhat leveled by the two half bricks under each corner where the legs should have been. The water supply, when it wasn't raining, came from an eighty-five foot dug well about fifteen feet from the kitchen door. This was covered by a shed roof which kept the water out of your hip pockets while you were pumping up your daily quota of H2O. The only time we had running water in the house was when it rained, which brought on an unbelievable orchestration of pots and pans and kettles, each with a distinctive tone."

Bob and Florence's unconventional honeymoon was a pack horse trip into the Blue Mountains of eastern Oregon, not a trip of Bob's choosing. After a few setbacks including getting lost, they arrived back in Chehalis somewhat disheveled to begin their life together. "He was a good sport about it," Florence said good-naturedly.

Tall, willowy and blue-eyed, the school teacher walked into the house on Kennicott Hill and into an unconventional life and marriage that would last for 55 years.

Florence Day Kennicott was born December 12, 1900 in Newaygo, Michigan and grew up in Clarkston, Washington. She attended college in Walla Walla, and graduated from Emerson College in Boston, later becoming an actress on Broadway as well as acting in travelling "stock" companies for several years. Tiring of the constant travel, Florence became an English literature and drama teacher at Castilleja Girls' High School in Palo Alto, California. She returned to Washington State and taught high school English in Centralia before accepting a position at Oregon Teachers' College in LaGrande. Giving up her acting and teaching careers, she became Robert's best friend and the mother of their two children. In 1950 Florence became the Lewis County Superintendent of Schools, in which capacity she served until her retirement in 1963.

After their marriage, Bob, Florence and the children spent many years together in the old house on Kennicott Hill. It burned down in 1960. After Harriet died, Grandpa Guy Kennicott sold the original Kennicott home and hospital on State and Prindle and moved into the small house adjacent to the main house on Kennicott hill and lived there next to his son, daughter-in-law and grandchildren during the last years of his life.

The old country doctor. Let him pass, with his old horse, his saddle bags, his nasty powders and his meager equipment. His like will never be seen again. Yet in his day, how anxiously he was awaited, how well he was known, how profoundly he was trusted. They even knew the quick cloppity-clop of his old horse, and how their strained faces relaxed, and their eyes brightened as he entered the poor little room, bringing hope and good cheer. They loved that old doctor, with his homely face and brusque ways, and now he is gone. God bless him and rest his tired old bones. (Dr. Guy Kennicott's recollections, 1929.)

Several years later when Frances learned of her cancer, she left her employment and moved into the same small house as well. She never married. According to the family, none of the interested young men were deemed by her mother, Harriet, to be of sufficient stature or prospects to marry her. She died in 1952.

After raising the family, Bob and Florence retired and circled the globe three times between 1964 and 1975, later living in New Zealand, Australia and Spain for as long as a year at a time.

Bob tells what happened after they returned from one particular trip. "It was great to see the Statue of Liberty welcoming us home in a snowstorm. We had been gone for over a year and was it ever a joy to see our friends again and learn of how much they had missed us. When we met them on the streets or in shops of Chehalis or Centralia, it just did something to us when they asked if we had been sick or something—because they hadn't seen us for a couple of weeks."

They enjoyed their last years together until Bob's health problems made it necessary for them to move into a place where he could receive more care. Due to diabetic complications, he had to be confined to a wheelchair during his final days. He was most unhappy with this mode of transportation, preferring tractors, wagons, horses or trucks. You could see him coming down the hall at Olympics West Assisted Living in Olympia, Washington in his wheelchair with his "*Screw the Golden Years*" cushion clearly visible on his lap or tucked under his arm. His mother would not have approved.

Robert W. Kennicott died in Olympia on December 27, 1990 at the age of 86. Eventually Florence's daughter, Dorothy moved her mother closer to her home in California. Although Florence's vision and hearing worsened, she remained mentally sharp until the end of her long life. Florence passed away on Feb 27, 2007 in Elk Grove California at the age of 106.

Florence and Bob inspire me to this day. I will never forget them.

Their two children, Dorothy Martinez-Kennicott and Robert Day Kennicott and their children and grandchildren carry on the legacy of this man and his wife and those who came before him; carrying on his dreams as well as their own into the yet-to-be-written future. I am indebted to both of them for their support and assistance on this project, including their hospitality and the rare family photographs they so kindly shared for this book.

Life had never been easy for Little Lord Fauntleroy who spent three years in kindergarten and got booted out of many prestigious colleges even more times than that, but then there are no guarantees after all. The only sure thing is that it was a life worth living in spite of the obstacles, and anyone who knew Bob Kennicott, knew he lived his life with gusto and courage.

Robert William Kennicott came a long way from that shoebox.

STATISTICAL SHEET OF THE
KENNICOTT FAMILY

Guy William Kennicott, M.D.
Born in Chicago, IL January 29,1859
Graduated Northwestern University
Doctor of Medicine Degree, Rush Medical College 1885
Frontier doctor in Wisconsin, 1886
Set up practice in Union, WA (then Union City) 1889
Married Harriet Foster Black, August 3, 1892
Bought out practice of J.S. Herndon, M.D. in Chehalis, 1895
Pioneer doctor in Chehalis and Lewis County, 1895-1942
Built first hospital in Lewis County, 1903
Chehalis City Health Officer, 1918-1942
Died in Chehalis, WA, March 1944. Buried at Claquato Cemetery

Harriet Foster Black Kennicott
Born in West Hebron, NY, December 25, 1863
Graduated from Westminster College, Pennsylvania 1885
Moved to Union WA and taught school, 1891
Married Guy William Kennicott, August 3, 1892
Moved to Chehalis with husband and daughter, Frances, 1895
Principal and instructor in Chehalis High School, 1896-98
Managed Chehalis Hospital for a quarter of a century
Died in Chehalis, WA, March 22,1942. Buried at Claquato Cemetery

Frances Caroline Kennicott
Born in Union, WA June 29, 1893
B.A. from Reed College, Portland, OR 1915
M.A. from Columbia University, NY
Graduate studies at the University of Washington, 1941-42
Taught at Annie Wright Seminary, Tacoma
Taught in St. Nicholas School, Seattle
Taught in St. Hilda's School in Wu Chang, China, 1922-25
Died in Chehalis, WA 1952. Buried at Claquato Cemetery

Robert William Kennicott
Born in Chehalis, 1904
Bought ranch on what is now called Kennicott Hill, 1931
Married Florence Day, September 1935
Died, December 27, 1990

Two Children:
Dorothy Frances Kennicott, born 1936
Robert Day Kennicott, born 1938

Several grandchildren

ENDNOTES

* French Voyageur: Frenchmen who transported furs by canoe during the fur trade era.

* Dropsy: Now called edema; an abnormal accumulation of fluid beneath the skin producing swelling.

* G.A.R. Grand Army of the Republic: A fraternal organization of the veterans of the Civil War.

* mahout: An elephant keeper and driver from India and the East Indies.

* Sikh: Followers of Sikhism, originating in the 15th century in the Punjab region of South Asia. A Sikh is a follower/disciple of the Guru.

* IWW Industrial Workers of the World: an international labor organization known as the Wobblies and founded in 1905 claiming over 100,000 members at its peak in 1923.

* George: Hrehory Marinuk was born in the 1880's in a Russian village near what is now Belarus.

* White Russian refers to a Slavic people from Belarus, now an independent country ethnically close to the Russians and Ukrainians.

My books and e-books are available at www.calamityjan.com.

Email me at clamityjan@aol.com

The Carson Kids Mysteries
    ages 9-13
The Mystery of Five Finger Island
The Secret of Howling Cove
The Mystery of the Skull Rocks Mansion
The Mystery of the Cove Point Stallion
Shipwreck on Grizzly Island

The Ghostowners **History-Mysteries set in ghost towns of the West**
    ages 9-13
Goodbye God, I'm Going to Bodie (Bodie, California)
Ghost of Nighthawk (Nighthawk, Washington)
Shadow of Shaniko (Shaniko, Oregon)
The Haunted Horse of Gold Hill (Gold Hill, Nevada)

Calamity Jan and the Russian **A memoir/narrative nonfiction**

Prohibition, Prostitution and Presbyterian Pews, **by Robert W. Kennicott with Jan Pierson**